EVERYBODY'S
COMPUTER
FIX-IT BOOK

EVERYBODY'S COMPUTER FIX-IT BOOK

JOEL MAKOWER
AND EDWARD MURRAY

Illustrations by William Coulter

Quantum Press/Doubleday
Garden City, New York
1985

Library of Congress Cataloging in Publication Data
Makower, Joel, 1952–
Everybody's computer fix-it book.
Includes index.
1. Microcomputers—Maintenance and repair.
I. Murray, Edward (Edward Eugene) II. Title.
TK7887.M356 1985   621.3819′584   84-24885
ISBN 0-385-19661-X

ACKNOWLEDGMENTS

Credit is due the following individuals who contributed in many ways to the information contained in these pages: Jack Barse, manager of The Computer Store of McLean, Virginia (our apologies, Jack, for depicting computer salespeople as vampires); Scotty Buell, private and patient tutor of microcomputer hardware, who works as an electrical engineer for the federal government; Charles Ogren, Regional Service Manager of Wordplex, Inc., who provided considerable information on some of the tricks of the computer repair trade; William Graham and Ronald L. Askew, both of MetaFont, Inc., who openly attacked errors of style and substance in the early drafts of this book; Susan Arritt, who gathered information on manufacturers' warranties; Paul Aron, of Doubleday, and literary agent Raphael Sagalyn, who helped bring this book to the marketplace.

And, finally, from Ed: To my wife, Janet; daughters, Vicky and Charlotte; and son, Little Ed, who have allowed me untold hours of freedom with my digital toys.

CONTENTS

INTRODUCTION

The headlines tell the story: "Business Is Booming for Computer Repair Shops," reports *InfoWorld,* a weekly computer trade publication; "New Franchises—Computer Repair," heralds the front page of the San Francisco *Chronicle;* "The Exploding Market for Computer Repair Services," reads the headline in *Business Week.*

Indeed, now that the microcomputer revolution has reached homes and businesses across the land, a sobering reality is beginning to sink in. Computers are like tuning forks: When they work, they hum; when they don't, they're useless.

Most of the time, they work. As appliances, computers are generally more reliable than, say, a Mercury or a Maytag. It's said that if the integrated circuits in your computer work for the first ninety minutes, they'll work for years without failure. And with good reason: There are relatively few moving parts in a computer. Where parts do move—disk drives and printers, for example—is where a computer system is most vulnerable.

Inevitably, things go wrong. Whether due to abuse or to old age, computers need repairs and maintenance from time to time. Equally inevitable, problems will arise the very moment you simply can't live without your computer, whether for business or for pleasure. It's as certain as death and taxes.

Most problems aren't that serious—if you know what's wrong. Barring a major tragedy—such as accidently dumping a Pepsi on your printer or getting a precious floppy disk caught under the wheel of your desk chair—there are few problems that can't be solved by replacing a part here or removing some built-up gunk there. Most times, in fact, a "problem" isn't really a problem at all but a result of your misunderstanding how to do something— often the result of unreadable instruction manuals and salespeople who don't know any more about computers than is needed to get products out the door.

The anxiety and frustration caused by all this has resulted in the booming industry of computer repair and maintenance, as reported by the publications cited above. Already, personal computer repair is a billion-dollar-a-year industry, and the majority of personal computers in existence are less than two years old. More than a dozen firms are competing to become the household name in computer repair. The U.S. Bureau of Labor Statistics predicts that jobs for computer service technicians will grow by more than 150 percent during the last half of the 1980s, making the field one of the biggest opportunities in the country. There's good reason for the fierce competition: By the end of the 1980s, say the experts, the computer-fixing industry may gross $5 billion to $8 billion annually. That's your money and ours.

The saddest part is that much of this money will be spent on repairs that aren't much more complicated than hooking together stereo components. If you've got the smarts to get a computer up and running—particularly in light of the horrid state of computer instruction manuals—you certainly can clean your disk drives, install additional memory chips, configure printer cables, or do any of a dozen other tasks. And you won't even get your hands dirty.

That's what this book is all about—the basic repair and maintenance tasks that just about anyone can do on almost any computer. You need only a few tools, a bit of patience, and the desire to do it yourself. In the pages that follow, we'll show you how to keep a computer running and what to do when it's not. We'll show you how to evaluate your equipment's symptoms to diagnose a problem. We'll show you how to make certain repairs yourself and tell you what repairs should be left to the experts.

In the process, you'll learn more about your computer and save enough money to keep yourself in ribbons, disks, and fanfold paper for as long as you own your system. If you're a tinkerer like us, you may even have a bit of fun.

EVERYBODY'S COMPUTER FIX-IT BOOK

PART I

GETTING STARTED

1
WHAT'S WRONG
WITH MY COMPUTER?

You've bought a computer, own a screwdriver and a pair of pliers, and are totally baffled by your new machine. You don't know the difference between a bit and a byte and are scared to death to open the cover of your computer and look inside. Come along. This book was written with you in mind.

Computer repair is a strange field. Due to the high-tech simplicity of most personal computers, computer service technicians have been reduced to being "board swappers," ripping out suspected defective circuit boards and replacing them with new ones. If something is wrong, they insert a diagnostic disk in your machine and run it through its paces. At some point, the machine tells them what to replace. Got a problem with the disk drive? Replace the drive. Something wrong with the monitor? Replace it. A flaky chip? Put in a new one.

That's today's world of computer repair. You don't need to know much about electronics. In fact, you may be better-off with a degree in psychology or history. Computer repair is not a matter of electronic engineering; it's a matter of identifying problems and solving them.

If you go to a neighborhood TV repair shop, you are likely to find technicians more skilled than those working at a local computer store. You'll see the TV technicians playing with voltmeters, oscilloscopes, and wiring diagrams. Computer technicians may have these tools too, but chances are they are armed also with a diagnostic disk that automatically determines a problem and spells out exactly what to do about it.

This method of troubleshooting makes sense. These days, a disk drive costs about $200; a used, reconditioned drive is considerably less. It can take several hours to accurately diagnose a disk drive problem and correct it. At $75 an hour, it doesn't pay to have a technician monkeying around with a drive for more than a few minutes. If the drive is bad, it may be cheaper to remove it and replace it with a new or reconditioned one. On the other hand, there are a number of repair depots with all sorts of automated equipment that specialize in certain types of computers or in certain types of repairs. These folks may fix a drive for around $50, something a computer store technician can't do.

But you may be able to do it yourself for even less.

Can You Fix a Computer?

You know little or nothing about a computer, so how can you be expected to fix one? It's pretty straightforward. In fact, in most cases there is nothing wrong.

What? *Nothing wrong?*

That's right. One of the hardest lessons to learn about computers is that when something appears to be messed up, chances are very, very high that you've made some kind of error in running a program, in setting switches on a device (such as a printer or modem), or in hooking up something. This is a very difficult lesson to learn but one that anyone with computer experience can attest to as a fact of computerized life.

Don't feel dumb. Even the experts suffer from this problem—a problem aggravated by the careless and haphazard way most computer instruction manuals are thrown together. Compounding the problem is the fact that many manuals contain gross errors. Similarly, there are software packages with known, but unreported, bugs. There are books available that are filled with technically incorrect information. And computer magazines publish tons of inaccurate material, only some of which eventually gets corrected. In this environment, making a mistake is not only understandable, it's highly likely.

When you become a computer sophisticate, you'll still be guilty of accusing your machine of doing things it shouldn't be doing when, in fact, you are the guilty party. Everything will point to the machine—everything, that is, except the one dumb mistake you made. Get used to it now; it will happen over and over.

The first lesson to learn is that just because your trusty computer *appears* to have failed doesn't mean it really is on the fritz. Don't run off to a repair shop, where you may be hit with a minimum charge of $50 or more, not to mention the temporary (perhaps a week or more) loss of your computer. And don't start tearing your machine apart yourself—at least not without some basic knowledge.

Here's a tip: If you want to pin down exactly what is wrong with your computer, describe to someone precisely what you're trying to do, the steps you went through to do it, and how you've done everything correctly. Explain how you really know your stuff. You've been through this same thing a hundred times before. Explain step-by-step what you've done and how your computer has let you down in spite of all you've done for it. Show how meticulous you've been (and how hurt you are). This is generally all it takes to make a complete fool of yourself, as it suddenly dawns on you that you forgot some minor, but vital, detail.

This is what computer repair is all about. The necessary skills are easily acquired. As long as you can set yourself up for a mild (but temporary, we promise) case of embarrassment, you've got what it takes to repair your own machine.

As you see, most computer repairs have nothing to do with fixing the machine. In fact, after the first few weeks of ownership, when you may encounter a lot of problems, your major repair task will be preventive maintenance—taking steps to ensure that your equipment will operate reliably for as long as possible. Your printer and disk drive, because they have mechanical (as opposed to electronic) components, may be exceptions to this, requiring some actual adjustments or repairs from time to time. But the computer itself is a very reliable machine.

Want to get an idea of how often you can expect a computer to break down? Don't think of your car. Those mechanical beasts are subject to all kinds of wear and tear. Everything gets bumped around and worn down. With the darn thing traveling a mile a minute down a rainy highway, or traveling over potholes as it turns corners, no adjustment lasts more than a few months, if that long.

Instead, think of other commonly used appliances. When, for example, was the last time your refrigerator broke down? Probably not very recently, unless you acquired a rare lemon of a model. They can go on for years and years, humming quietly in the kitchen. This is what you should expect from your computer. With a little care, it can keep computing for years and years.

What You Can and Can't Do

Everything you'll find in the section on preventive maintenance is well within the abilities of just about anyone. That's because most of what you will do to avoid problems is to *not* do things that can threaten your equipment. When it comes to repairs, you'll have to be the judge of what you feel comfortable with.

The level of repair presented in this book can be handled easily by anyone able to follow a few simple instructions. But if you don't feel right about it, you are probably better-off not trying.

Forget about wiring diagrams, schematic drawings, oscilloscopes, and other complicated things electronic. Common sense is a better tool to help you find your way to a bad board or other component. Example: To solve a minor but aggravating problem, you may need only to remove a bad circuit board from its socket, clean it, and inspect it for obvious damage—a bad solder joint or a burned-out area, for example. Then stick it back in. If that doesn't fix what's wrong, borrow a similar board from a friend and see if the machine runs right. If it does, you know there's something wrong with the board itself. This is what many repairs are all about. As with those high-priced computer repair technicians mentioned earlier, the "fix" typically involves simply replacing something.

Getting the Diagnosis

What all this comes down to is that, with a modicum of effort, you have virtually the same chance of repairing your machine as a service rep at a computer store, although you may need a few tools and maybe a diagnostic disk. Diagnostic disks are available for most machines, although some manufacturers provide them only to authorized service technicians. The necessary tools range in price from under $1.00 to more than $100 and may or may not be worth having. (In Chapter 3, under Everybody's Fix-It Tool Kit, page 34, we'll show you how to put together a perfectly adequate tool kit for about $50, the typical minimum charge for bringing your computer into a shop.) If you've blown a disk drive, the central processing unit, or your monitor, the various diagnostic disks on the market won't do you much good anyway—they depend on the operation of these critical components to run their tests.

The diagnostic tools are of limited value in other ways. Example: For around $35 you can buy IBM's *Hardware Maintenance and Service Manual* for the Personal Computer model, complete with diagnostic disks and two "loop-back" plugs for testing communications. To the extent that your system is running well enough to let you operate this program, it provides a method for locating problems. There is, however, little information on what to do about a problem, other than to replace the faulty component. It's hard to justify the expense for something like this unless you plan to go into the computer repair business.

At the other extreme, the folks at Tandy Corporation, makers of Radio Shack computers, provide a number of technical reference manuals with step-by-step instructions for troubleshooting problems. The manuals provide complete schematics and parts lists, but they aren't accompanied by a diagnostic disk. Compared with IBM, you have a lot more information, but you must be quite knowledgeable to make good use of it.

Somewhere in the middle is Apple Computer, which has chosen to limit distribution of its manuals and other diagnostic tools to its authorized dealers. However, a number of products from independent companies are available to Apple computer owners. The problem is that most of these are not particularly comprehensive—they amount to little more than a collection of programs that permit analysis of a limited number of disk drive-related problems.

The Joy of Joining

Besides the diagnostic routines available directly from manufacturers or independent software houses, you can find some limited diagnostic packages floating around in the public domain, usually available through users' groups.

There are many reasons for joining a users' group for your machine. One big reason is the help you can get to keep your machine up and running. The $15 to $25 annual membership fee most groups charge may be worth many times that amount, especially when you consider the cost of a diagnostic package or a single repair bill.

Equally important, membership will put you in touch with others who may be valuable allies in your battle to keep your computer computing. In addition to getting good advice through a users' group, you may also get assistance in the form of loaned components that may help you diagnose problems, as well as information on common problems you are likely to run into. Also helpful are the contacts and information you may develop, which can steer you to competent and reasonably priced service when you run into problems beyond your capabilities to fix. A good service engineer at a local service store may belong to a users' group; other competent part-time or free-lance technicians also can be found among the ranks of users' group members.

There's more. A users' group may collectively invest in various diagnostic tools, which can be loaned to members having problems. Having use of a $150 diagnostic disk is a lot cheaper than buying one for your own very limited use. Similarly, an oscilloscope can be a very handy tool for pinning down computer problems but is much too expensive for the typical user's tool kit.

No matter how you look at it, joining a users' group will pay handsome dividends, including providing you with the kind of up-to-date product-specific information and support that is beyond the scope of this book.

The Crucial First Few Months

When you first get your computer, the most important thing for you to do is "burn it in." (See Before the Warranty Runs Out, page 10.) This will help you locate any weak components in your system and get them replaced while the system is still under warranty. If your computer survives this burn-in period, chances are good that, with proper care, it will last a lifetime, or almost.

During the warranty period, you shouldn't attempt any repairs yourself. While it may be inconvenient to pack up your machine and carry or send it to a repair shop, you should do this anyway. For one thing, repair costs will be borne by the manufacturer while a machine is under warranty. Second, if you foul up an attempted repair, you'll probably have to foot the repair bill, even though the machine is under warranty.

When the warranty runs out, you may get a service contract—in effect, an extended warranty. (See Chapter 13 for more on service contracts and warranties.) This is a tough choice for many computer owners because the cost of service contracts is usually high—typically about 5 percent to 20 percent of the value of your system per year. On a $3,000 system, that's $150 to $600. If your machine is being used for business on a daily basis and any extended unavailability would create a great hardship, you probably have no choice but to go the service contract route.

If, on the other hand, you are simply using your machine for personal purposes and a few days' breakdown wouldn't matter much, you can probably safely choose to provide your own maintenance, with back-up service provided by a competent dealer or independent service organization. (You may wish to consider setting aside the money you save by not getting a service contract in an informal "service account" to cover expenses you may have from time to time.)

A Good Shop Is Hard to Find

No matter which course you choose, you should develop a good relationship with a repair shop. In some cases this may be

Before
the Warranty
Runs Out

In the old days, electronic equipment manufacturers built their equipment, put it in a hot room for a couple weeks, and then ran it through its paces. This was known as "burning it in." While this wasn't a foolproof method of uncovering a machine's weaknesses, it was quite effective. The reason? Heat makes weak parts fail.

These days, the demand for most components far exceeds the supply. For many manufacturers, burning-in is a thing of the past. A manufacturer's products are likely to be sold months before they even hit an assembly line. A computer store will assemble the components you purchased and may leave them on overnight, but that's about it.

This means that you'll have to do the burn-in yourself, before the warranty expires. What you must do is turn the machine on and leave it on for several weeks. This gives any weak components an opportunity to burn out on the manufacturer's nickel, not yours.

Occasionally during the burn-in period, turn the machine off, then on, several times in a row. If there is a weak component, this will probably cause it to go.

the dealer from which you purchased your machine or one of the many independent service organizations springing up around the country. But you may find an independent free-lancer who can provide you with the same level of service at a much lower cost. (A users' group, as we said earlier, is a good place to look.) Your choice in this regard is a function of what you feel comfortable with and what resources are available. (See Chapter 12 for more on finding good repair shops.)

Must you absolutely use a repair shop? Probably not. There is no reason why you can't do everything yourself, or at least a large portion of it. But even if you feel comfortable handling your computer's innards, you are likely to find it much more effective if you work with a repair shop. While you may be capable of pinpointing a problem, getting a replacement part is not always easy, except by going through an authorized service center for your machine. This isn't to say you *can't* get the part, just that it can be difficult.

Say, for example, you break the door on your disk drive. What's wrong is very obvious and how to replace it pretty straightforward. You are likely to find, however, that the disk drive manufacturer is not all that interested in dealing with you, a mere retail customer, who wants to buy one replacement door. You'll even run into situations where a component supplier has an agreement with a computer manufacturer that specifically prohibits the manufacturer from selling directly to "end users," as they're known in the business.

While the latter kind of arrangement might be open to legal challenge, the former makes sense. Few manufacturers of anything like to deal directly with customers. They'd much rather make their deals with distributors and wholesalers. This lets them keep their overhead low and focus on doing what they do best—manufacturing.

Wholesalers aren't much better than manufacturers when it comes to dealing with computer owners. Again, this is as it should be. Unfortunately, there just aren't a lot of retail computer part suppliers, even in big cities. Sure, there are electronics shops, even computer part stores, and some have enormous inventories. But chances are that something like a disk drive door for your particular model won't be in stock. In some cases they'll order a part for you, but you may need to be a pretty good customer to get such service.

This is why it pays to develop a relationship with a dealer or independent repair shop. They can get the parts you need. More important, they can probably get them quickly and in a way that will actually save you money.

"Field Replaceable Units"

As we said before, it is entirely possible for you to make any repair to your machine, right down to individual circuit components. The problem is being able to isolate problems at this level, then remove a component that is soldered to a circuit board. It can be done, but even skilled technicians don't like doing it.

When you examine the economics of computer repair, you'll see it really pays to attempt some repairs only if you are a specialized repair depot, fixing only IBM PC disk drives, for example, or if you're the original manufacturer. These folks can afford to put together automated test equipment for isolating problems and to set up the necessary equipment for replacing bad components.

Again, you could troubleshoot on your own, desolder a bad chip, and install a replacement, but chances are you won't be able to easily isolate a problem down to this level or, having accomplished this, be able to remove the defective component and replace it without risking messing up something else in the process.

Dealers, independent repair facilities, even manufacturer's service facilities do their repairs at the "field replaceable unit" level. Translated, this means the smallest item that can be replaced easily outside a full-service shop—"in the field," in the parlance of repair folks—is an entire circuit board, for example, a complete disk drive, or a similar subsystem. (This is agonizingly similar to the notion of "rip and replace," popular among car mechanics.) Example: A field service engineer or the technician at the local computer store will clean disk drive heads. He or she may even adjust the drive's timing. Beyond that, the technician probably will simply pull a poorly working disk drive and replace it. The pulled drive will be sent to a specialized repair facility or back to the manufacturer, where the necessary troubleshooting and repair facilities exist.

So it doesn't make a lot of sense for you to try to make repairs at a level beyond that of more skilled and better-equipped technicians. There are some exceptions to this rule, but for the most part, what you'll do is take steps to prevent problems, make a few repairs and adjustments, and provide a good set of diagnostics to make this task as easy (and as inexpensive) as possible for a technician.

Repair Secrets

While a computer may appear to you to be a mysterious black (or gray or white or green) plastic (usually) box, there are a few tricks to keeping it up and running that will work 90 percent of the time you *think* you have a problem.

We said it before, and we'll say it once again: Most of the time you think your trusty computer is on the blink, the problem has nothing to do with your machine. You simply have done something wrong—or at least haven't done something right. It matters not that you've done something similar successfully before—you can still make mistakes.

Here are three tricks of the trade:

* When something seems to be haywire, make sure you are really doing everything right and have all wires and switches set properly. Double or triple check this, especially if you are doing something new. Your printer doesn't seem to work now that you've installed a new program? Make sure you set everything up properly—both on the program and on the printer. If it still doesn't work, try something you *know* should work and see if you still have a problem.

* Your next step, having firmly established that you aren't doing something wrong, is to move things around a bit. There's no logic to this at all, just a gut feeling. The fact is, flaky components like to be moved. Turn the machine off. If you can isolate a problem down to the level of a circuit board, remove the board and stick it back in. Only the great God of Electrons knows why this works, but it does.

  An IBM PC, one of the many IBM compatibles, an Apple, and other microcomputers with option slots provide repeated opportunities for proving the move-it theory. Try it yourself. Take a PC, run a diagnostic routine, and firmly establish that you have a bad board. Then pull the board and stick it right back where it came from, and you'll find nine times out of ten you've fixed the problem. If that doesn't work, simply move the board to another slot and—*presto*—you're one notch below a fully qualified service engineer. What probably happens is that a board has a tendency to work itself loose or to get its contacts gooped up to the point where the appropriate signals aren't getting through. Removing the board and putting it back in place may be all you need to restore the necessary contact.

* A similar phenomenon occurs when you've hooked something up incorrectly or made some sort of error in running a program or an operating system command. If you were to go through the effort, you'd probably find that a diagnostic routine would reveal some kind of "fatal" hardware failure. Doing a "soft" reset (resetting your computer without turning the machine off) or even shutting the machine off and turning it back on may not be enough to clear the error. But if you shut it off and leave it off for thirty seconds or so, hocus-pocus, the problem disappears. You won't find the answer to such mysteries in circuit diagrams, although there are components that will retain settings in spite of resetting your system or turning your power off for a minute or more. How this process works is probably beyond our abilities to fathom. But it works, and if it does, you're a repair genius. Accept it on faith.

Let's Get Going

If you've come this far, you should be thoroughly convinced that you—the complete, all-thumbs novice—are capable of maintaining and repairing your own computer. You can't do everything yourself, nor should you—the experts don't do everything either. Millions of ordinary folks routinely maintain and repair their own cars, contraptions far more complicated and complex than a computer. Besides being easier than repairing cars, working on computers is a lot less messy. You won't get coated with grease or cut up your hands.

How far you go is pretty much up to you. You must at all times maintain a very, very healthy regard for the hazards of electricity. (See Future Shock, page 16.) While it is true that most voltages in a computer are harmless and that electrically you are more of a threat to your computer (from static electricity) than it is to you, you shouldn't take chances. (See Zapping Delicate Circuits, page 51.) With the exception of procedures that require power, such as adjusting disk drive timing, always disconnect a computer before attempting any preventive maintenance or repair operation. And don't just turn the power off—*unplug the machine.*

We should note a little conflict here. When you unplug your machine, you no longer have a true ground. This can result in problems with static electricity. It's a toss-up, but we strongly advise that you opt for unplugging the machine to be certain the power is off, but you must be very careful about static electricity.

You will find a natural hesitancy to do anything on your computer when it is new to you—even running a new program. There is a fear that you might mess things up. As you grow more familiar with your computer, you'll find the fear disappearing. You will still make mistakes, lose a file or two, or lock your system up so tightly that only Houdini could break it loose, but you will come to realize that such things are inevitable and can quickly be set straight.

The same is true of computer maintenance and repair. Initially, you'll be scared to death that you are going to do something terribly wrong. This is always possible, but as you develop a feel for your machine and see that your actions don't bring instant doom, you'll begin to feel more confident—ready to tackle anything. You may not want to rip out circuit boards or tear your printer apart when you are just beginning to get to know your machine, but you are certainly capable of taking a vacuum cleaner and blowing the dust and grime out of your computer. Go ahead and do this, and leave the other jobs to the pros. Eventually, you'll be comfortable enough to do a lot more.

Ease into it. There are no savings in going ahead when you're afraid that every step is going to ruin your computer or result in a life-threatening shock. Plunging in and taking responsibility for its maintenance is fun, challenging, and educational. You will

Future Shock

Electricity kills. Don't play around with it. Saving a few bucks isn't worth it if you zap yourself in the process. Fortunately, with the exception of the power supply and CRT, there is very little electricity in a microcomputer. We're talking about 5 and 12 volts in most cases—about the amount of power it takes to run a flashlight.

Even so, components such as the monitor can be hazardous, even though the operating voltage may be only 12 volts DC. The monitor acts like a capacitor, storing a charge that can be in the neighborhood of 10,000 volts or more. That charge can be there *even if your computer is unplugged.* A jolt of this magnitude probably wouldn't kill you if you are a healthy young athlete, but it might if you have a heart problem and, regardless of your health, it would make your hair stand up—and make you very, very shy about poking around your machine.

In most of a computer's system, you are more of a threat to it than it is to you. Merely coming near some components when you are charged with static is enough to zap many delicate integrated circuits.

But you still must be careful about getting zapped yourself. There is simply no reason to take chances. Rule Number One is: Before you open your computer, *disconnect the power.* Sure it's turned off, but it's not necessarily harmless.

save yourself a buck or two, which you probably can put to better use.

Take your time. You can do it. It just takes a little while to get familiar with things.

2
TROUBLESHOOTING GUIDE

Symptom	Possible Culprit	*See* *Chapter*
	GENERAL	
Computer won't run	No AC power coming from household outlet	4, 10
	Computer not turned on	
	Fuse blown in computer	
	Power supply defective	
	Poorly soldered circuit board connection	
	Short circuit	
	On/off switch broken	
Computer runs, but locks up	Fluctuation in power supply	3, 4, 10
	Operating system defective	
	Lightning	
	Microprocessor defective	
	Memory chip defective	
	Memory chip loose	
	Overheating	
	Power supply fluctuation	
	Scratched circuit board	
	Static electricity	
	Loose circuit board	
	Dirt or dust on circuit board	
	Operator error	
Occasional logic error	Defective component	3, 4
	Short circuit	
	Overheating	
	Static electricity	
	Dirt or dust on circuit board	
	Microprocessor defective	

Symptom	Possible Culprit	See Chapter
DISK DRIVES		
Drives not operating	Bad cable connection	3, 5, 10
	Defective drive motor	
	Defective disk controller	
Drive runs, but won't properly read or write data	Bad disk in drive	
	Dirty read/write head	
	Drive timing off	
	Drive alignment off	
	Defective disk controller	
	Electrical interference	
	Overheating	
	Static electricity	
MONITOR		
Character displays poorly	Bad character ROM chip	4, 9
Portion of screen displays poorly	Bad video RAM chip	
	Short or open circuit on LCD	

Note: We recommend you not attempt further troubleshooting or repair of CRTs.

	KEYBOARD	
Keyboard doesn't work	Not connected to CPU	3, 4, 7
	Defective cable or plug	
	Defective key switch	
	Defective keyboard ROM chip	
Key works, but isn't correct	Defective key circuit	
Key sticks	Dirty or defective key switch	
Key repeats excessively	Untuned debounce circuit	

| *Symptom* | *Possible Culprit* | *Chapter* |

MODEM

Symptom	Possible Culprit	See Chapter
Modem doesn't work	Bad cable connection	6, 8
	Improper switch setting	
	Improper software setting	
	Defective modem	
Modem works, but communication garbled	Improper switch setting	
	Improper software setting	
	Bad cable connection	
	Improper cable wiring	
	Dirty circuit board (plug-in modem only)	
	Improper communications protocol	
	Defective interface circuit	
	Intermittent short or open circuit	

PRINTER

Symptom	Possible Culprit	See Chapter
Printer not working	Bad cable connection	4, 6, 11
	Improper cable wiring	
	Improper switch setting	
	Improper software setting	
	Defective interface circuitry	
	Defective control circuitry	
	Dust or dirt on circuit board	
Printer works, but alignment off	Loose horizontal positioning belt	
	Defective positioning motor	
Printer works, but copy missing or garbled	Improper switch setting	
	Defective character ROM chip	
	Loose cable	
	Defective printer memory	
Image too light	Ribbon worn-out	
	Defective or dirty print head assembly	
	Ribbon too tight	
Characters broken	Print wheel broken or not inserted properly	
Characters smudged	Ribbon too loose	

3
PREVENTIVE MAINTENANCE

We all know that preventing a problem is better than fixing it after it occurs. It's usually easier and cheaper, too. Human nature being what it is, however, we rarely practice this. We know we shouldn't smoke and eat junk food, but we do. Then we demand that our doctors perform miracles to cure the ills caused by our bad habits. We expect our car mechanics to fix in an hour or two what resulted from months or years of abuse and neglect.

Not surprisingly, we do the same thing to our computers. If it survives the first month or so of operation, it can go on happily computing forever (or almost) if you merely take a few simple steps to maintain its health. If, on the other hand, you abuse your trusty machine, swear at it when it collapses under this abuse, then complain when the local technician can't bring it back to life instantly, you have only yourself to blame.

Nothing in this book will change human nature. Optimists that we are, however, we'll nevertheless share on the following pages the rituals we follow that can lead to healthy lives for computers.

A Healthy Computer

Your computer, having evolved (more or less) from humans, demands almost the same environmental conditions that you do. For example:

* A computer doesn't like to be too hot or too cold. It differs a
    bit from humans in that it does prefer cool to warm, but it

tolerates either. (Some humans are like this, too; computers must have evolved from this branch of the species.)

* Much as we prefer not to be stifled, a computer finds life a bit uncomfortable when its air vents are blocked and assorted objects are piled on top of, under, and behind it. The more air and elbow room it has, the better.
* Polluted air is anathema to the health of both computers and humans; it tends to rot the innards of both.
* Smoking is a no-no for humans and computers. Abuse your lungs and your computer at the risk of both.
* You would not function well if you were confined to a dank, damp basement. Neither will a computer.

One clear evolutionary advance over humans exhibited by a computer is its total rejection of junk food. Not only doesn't it like hamburgers, with or without special sauce, it can't stomach soft drinks, french fries, or any other dietary delights. When you get right down to it, it will reject all food, in the forms we humans have come to know it.

Your computer consumes electricity and prefers that it be steady and reliable. It also accepts most floppy disks but asks that they be as clean as humans are capable of making them.

While somewhat fanatic about cleanliness, it hasn't come to appreciate the joys and relaxation of water. In fact, computers don't like water, period. Its equivalent of a long, hot shower is being blasted with clean air that blows away dust and grit. It seems to especially like really concentrated blasts aimed at specific places. Like humans, it gets funky if it goes too long between "baths."

That's it. It's not much more than we ask for ourselves. To have a happy computer, all that's required is that you do for it what you would have it do for you. But hold the mayo.

A Clean Machine

Most of preventive maintenance involves keeping your computer clean and free of hazards like dust, liquids, and food.

If you live in a city or in nearby suburbs, you know too well how quickly dust and other airborne stuff can build up. While your computer may appear well protected from this, in fact it is not.

The screen of a CRT *attracts* airborne particles. Judging by what accumulates inside most computers, the circuit boards also seem to have this affinity for dirt.

A dust cover over your machine—as simple as a worn-out old sheet—helps keep it clean when you're not using it. You should also dust off the machine at least as regularly as you dust off your window sills. (Probably even better, you should dust your computer as often as your mother dusts *her* window sills.)

PREVENTIVE MAINTENANCE

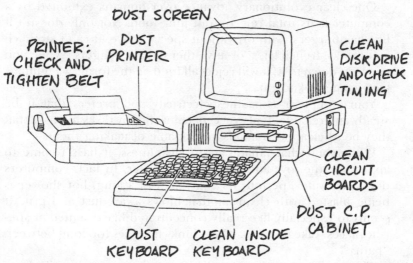

DUST SCREEN

PRINTER: CHECK AND TIGHTEN BELT

DUST PRINTER

CLEAN DISK DRIVE AND CHECK TIMING

CLEAN CIRCUIT BOARDS

DUST C.P. CABINET

DUST KEYBOARD   CLEAN INSIDE KEYBOARD

A damp, not wet, cloth is all that's necessary. You needn't buy any magic sprays or potions. A clean rag and a few drops of water will do the trick. If you let things get out of hand and the dust turns into unsightly grime, you'll need to add ammonia to water —a couple capfuls of ammonia to a quart of water—to clean the metal or plastic surfaces of your computer. You also can use commercial window-cleaning products, but don't spray them directly on the computer—spray them on your cleaning rag.

The more often you do this, the less chance your shiny machine

An Ounce
of Prevention

Here's a preventive maintenance checklist to help you stay current on your computer cleaning chores.

Once a week:
Dust off the entire system—screen, keyboard, central processor cabinet, and printer, including as much of the printer's insides as you can get to easily. If you have a fan with a filter, the filter should be cleaned weekly.

Once a month:
Clean out inside the keyboard. Examine the printer's belts for tightness.

Once every two months:
Clean the printer's print head. Clean the printer's insides thoroughly. Clean the disk drive read/write heads.

Once every six months:
Check disk drive alignment. Clean the circuit boards.

will take on a filthy look. Moreover, by getting rid of the dust on the outside, you'll save yourself having to get it out of the inside.

By the way, your mother dusts at least once a week.

Between the Keys

While most of your computer may seem well protected by its cabinet, many keyboards—particularly the common typewriter-style keyboards—are very much exposed.

If you do nothing to keep the keyboard clean, it will eventually accumulate all sorts of gunk, dust, and a few crumbs. You'd be surprised how much hair, paper clips, and assorted other material can find its way between the keys.

Many keyboard designs have gone a long way to protect the individual switches that constitute the innards of a keyboard. If you don't have one of these designs, chances are you will foul things up if you don't clean the keyboard out fairly frequently, probably monthly.

You have a couple of choices. You can run a vacuum cleaner over the keyboard—with the computer turned off—or you can buy a can of compressed air (about $4.00) from a photo supply shop. You can save yourself this expense by putting your vacuum in reverse and using it to blow the dirt out of the keyboard.

You needn't take anything apart to do this. Just hold the keyboard upside down, aim the vacuum nozzle, and blow it out. If, on the other hand, you are just getting started in the repair business (and you have a keyboard that detaches from the rest of the computer), go ahead and take it apart, but make sure the power is off first. Disassembly is generally quite simple—three or four screws are all that hold it together. There may be a plug where the keyboard cable attaches to the keyboard, which you should disconnect if you want a little more freedom to remove the keyboard's circuit board. By the way, while you have it opened for cleaning, explore the wonders of its circuitry.

Repairs are a lot easier once you get over fearing the unknown. The more you take your machine apart, if for no other reason than to look at what's going on inside, the more comfortable you'll begin to be with troubleshooting and repairs. And anytime you go to the trouble of opening up some component, go ahead and clean it.

A Clean Screen

As mentioned earlier, dust, grease, and grime are attracted to a CRT screen. This isn't particularly harmful to a computer, although it can build up to the point where it can harm you. If you are straining to read the screen, you're a candidate for eyestrain, headaches, a sore back, and a host of other "terminal" illnesses.

Cleaning the screen is no different from cleaning other computer surfaces except you'll probably need a wetter rag. Plain water doesn't cut through the grime, so it may help to add a couple capfuls of ammonia per quart of water. Any commercial window cleaner will do just fine.

Paper Tigers

The federal government launched a totally unsuccessful campaign against paper in the mid 1970s. Our nation's leaders didn't realize that, with the microcomputer revolution, the rest of us were preparing an assault on the nation's forests several orders of magnitude greater than any bureaucracy dared dream possible. Indeed, the truth about the "paperless society" brought about by computers is that, what with high-speed printers, we'll print out something without a minute's hesitation, then make a small change and print it out again. And again and again. The result: We use more paper than ever before.

With all that paper comes paper dust. Not only is it a threat to your printer's well-being, it somehow has a knack for finding its way into every nook and cranny in your entire computer system. You must stop it at the source—the printer. Even if you don't clean the rest of your computer system frequently, you *must* clean the printer. If you fail, count on it getting gummed up—and risk the rest of the system being brought down by it.

Use common sense. It isn't easy to get into all the cracks and crevices of a printer, even with a long, narrow vacuum attachment. You'll probably have to blow some of it out with compressed air or a reversed vacuum. But you won't have accomplished much if you just blow it out of the printer and it flies around the room, landing on your computer. Throw a sheet—the one you use to cover the computer during off-hours—over the computer and anything else you want to spare from dust. Better yet, if it isn't too much trouble, take the printer outside, or at least out of the computer room. The goal is to get rid of the paper dust, not spread it around.

We'll Drink to That

Accidents happen, and chances are that someday you'll spill something on your computer or disks. It may seem relatively harmless—a glass of water, perhaps—but it can damage your equipment in a big way.

You probably already know that water and electricity don't mix, so the first thing you must worry about when you spill something on your computer is the potential for electric shock. Your first action (after you make sure that whatever you spilled has stopped running into your computer) is to unplug everything.

The severity of the incident depends partly on what and how much was spilled. The worst problems come with liquids containing acids—most soft drinks, for example. The carbonic acid in a soft drink is mild, to be sure, but it will do a real number on the metal in your machine. The next biggest problem is with drinks containing sugar. After the liquid dries, the sugar remains, leaving a sticky, scratchy mess that can really foul things up.

Many computer components are hardy enough to withstand a quick dunking. If the liquid spilled was water—even hot water in the form of coffee or tea with no cream or sugar—you can get by with blotting up what liquids you can see, then blowing it dry with a hair dryer or a vacuum cleaner in

Around the Circuit

Cleaning the circuit boards inside the computer should be done with care. There's no reason to touch anything, and you shouldn't use a cloth. The only liquid you should consider using is alcohol or electrical-contact/relay cleaner. But these liquids should be used only in extreme cases—such as a spill. (See We'll Drink to That, above.)

reverse. Worry a bit about overheating your components with the hair dryer, but getting it dry quickly is more important.

If you spilled a soft drink or some other sticky liquid, you've got to get it off. Probably the safest approach is to try cleaning it with electrical-contact/relay cleaner, although it's rather expensive and may not give you enough liquid to wash things off thoroughly. Another approach is to literally bathe the board with isopropyl (rubbing) alcohol. Be sure it's straight alcohol—no sweet-smelling additives are needed by your computer. Be careful—it's flammable. But it dries quickly and shouldn't cause any real problems. And it's cheaper than electrical contact cleaner and probably more effective.

Disk drives are another problem. If one got drenched, you probably should have it professionally cleaned, lubricated, and realigned. Foreign matter that gets into the drive could cause it to scratch disks.

If you got disks wet, you're probably better off tossing them out and hoping that you've got backup copies. You can try wiping them off, but if moisture or other foreign matter remains, you run the risk of ruining a disk drive when you insert the soiled disk into your machine. If the disks got by with only a sprinkling, let them dry thoroughly (the lining in which disks are housed is absorbent, so let it dry overnight), then try reading one file. If you're successful, copy all the files from one disk to another and throw away the original.

And thank your lucky stars.

There's only one proven circuit board-cleaning method: blowing the dust out. You'll find the major concentration of dust around the fan. If there is an accumulation, think carefully about where the dust will go when you blow it; try to figure out a way to have it blow clear of the machine.

Concentrate the air blast around computer chips. Any socket or connection—whether for a plug-in board, peripheral interface, or socketed IC—should get special attention because dust tends to build up, particularly on the "female" side of the connection. If you choose to use a reversed vacuum, keep the vacuum cleaner itself far away from the computer to avoid possible static problems. (Static can permanently damage a board.) Be very careful about poking the nozzle attachment around. You want to reach all those out-of-the-way spots, but not at the expense of banging something loose.

CLEANING A CIRCUIT BOARD

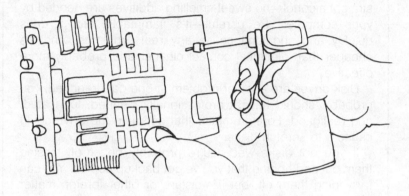

A Plea

Try to set up a computer maintenance schedule and to keep a log to remind you when it's time for something to be done. (See the sample maintenance log on page 32.) We know it's no fun doing maintenance, especially when you could be playing *Space Invaders* or creating spreadsheets. But the inevitable price of neglect is a computer failure (perhaps just when you're about to defeat the dratted invaders or to compute your final calculations). It always occurs at the wrong time (it's a law of computing), and it may cost you a bundle to set things straight.

Keeping Logs

It used to be that only ships' captains kept logs, which ended up as parts of seafaring novels. But logs can help computer owners keep their heads above water, too. Among other things, they'll get you to organize your computing life and to document important information that you can keep in one place. You can keep your logs on computer, of course, so you can update them whenever necessary. It's a good idea to keep printed versions in a safe place so that you'll have information that can facilitate repairs when your computer isn't working.

Here are three logs you should consider keeping:

Problem Log

You can save yourself hours of troubleshooting up dark alleys if you keep a systematic problem log. (We have included a sample on page 30. You should enter the form on your word processor so you can keep this and other logs on computer.) Basically, the log should be a journal of all problems you are having, including as many details as possible: date and time, exactly what software you're using, what you were doing or trying to do when the problem arose, environmental conditions, and the exact nature of the problem. If you found a solution, however temporary, that, too, should be noted.

Your problem log should be a permanent part of your computer documentation. By maintaining the log, not only will you have a quick way to see if there is a pattern to a problem, you'll also have a picture of subtle problems that build up over time. Be sure to note both specific symptoms of as well as general environmental conditions during problems, because both are important in tracing a problem's source.

Be liberal in recording problems, even if you don't think they are necessarily hardware-related. Such a record may help convince you that most problems are not the fault of the machine itself, and, on the brighter side, you'll have a written record of how smart you have become as you see the problems occurring less and less frequently.

PROBLEM LOG

Symptom   *Date*   *Action Taken*

_____

_____

_____

_____

_____

_____

_____

_____

_____

_____

_____

_____

_____

_____

_____

_____

_____

_____

_____

_____

_____

_____

_____

_____

_____

_____

_____

_____

_____

_____

_____

_____

_____

_____

_____

_____

_____

_____

_____

Maintenance Log

Your maintenance log is a vital piece of record keeping for your computer system. (We have included a sample on page 32.) By keeping your maintenance log up to date, you'll have a constant reminder that can prod you into doing the routine preventive maintenance that will keep your computer up and running. Equally important, you'll have a record of anything you've done that may have caused a problem.

Your maintenance log will also provide you with good documentation of the care you have lavished on your computer should you need that kind of information when you take your equipment in for service. If you decide to sell your computer, the impressive log of your constant attention will enhance your machine's value.

Parts Log

Getting replacements for defective parts is a lot easier if you maintain a parts log. (We have included a sample on page 33.) You should record basic information on each component of your computer that you purchase separately. This will make it easier to get in touch with the manufacturer, if necessary, as well as provide you with the vital part numbers you'll need to obtain service or replacement. If you record prices as well, you'll also have a good record of how much your computer has cost. That may come in handy at tax time, if you deduct business use of your computer from your taxes. By keeping track of retailers and distributors you deal with, you'll have a ready reference to possible sources of parts.

Finally, and perhaps most important, your parts log serves as a quick reference for warranty information by allowing you to keep tabs on when you purchased various components. Helpful as the log may be in this regard, don't forget to send off your equipment's warranty registration card. You may not qualify for warranty service if you don't do this. Moreover, sending in your registration card will ensure that the manufacturer can get in touch with you if it uncovers a problem with the product or offers subsequent enhancements to it.

MAINTENANCE LOG

Date	Action	Approximate Cost

PARTS LOG

Part Description	Serial Number	Date Acquired	Where Purchased	Manufacturer Address/Phone

Everybody's Fix-It Tool Kit

Maintaining and repairing a computer requires very few tools. You'll probably find you already have most things you need—a screwdriver and pair of pliers, for example. Add a few cotton swabs and a bottle of isopropyl (rubbing) alcohol—both available at drugstores for under $2.00—and a vacuum cleaner that permits you to blow air, and you've got most of what you really need to do many of the tasks you'll encounter. The complete tool kit, however, should include a few additional items.

Small Is Beautiful. Having the right tool always makes a job easier. A big, clunky screwdriver may be fine for prying a door open, but you may find it awkward to use inside your computer. The same is true with pliers. You'll find that smaller tools do the job better than those you typically use around the house. You may want to invest in a set of three different-size screwdrivers (both flat and Phillips head) and a similar range of pliers, including one small needle-nose pair. A nut driver with various-size sockets can be useful in reaching nuts that pliers can't.

Multimeter. A multimeter—a device used to measure voltage and circuit resistance—can be one of the handiest items around. You can buy one for about $15 to $30. There are two types, digital and analog; digital is easier to use by a novice. A multimeter isn't vital, but it can be useful when it comes to troubleshooting problems involving cables. Moreover, it can be used for other things around the house, including checking your car's battery.

Vacuum Cleaner. A vacuum cleaner that permits you to reverse the hose so you can blow air is a very useful tool. You may find some very good ones on the market for $50 or less, especially if you hit a yard sale or two. You don't need one just for your computer, of course; it can be used for general vacuuming, too. To be effective, it should have a crevice attachment (a long, narrow nozzle). You may wish to put tape over part of the opening to create a more concentrated blast of air. Another good source of compressed air comes in cans, about $4.00 a can. Such products come with the tiny nozzles needed to get into tight spaces. You'll find them useful for a variety of things.

EVERYBODY'S FIX-IT TOOL KIT

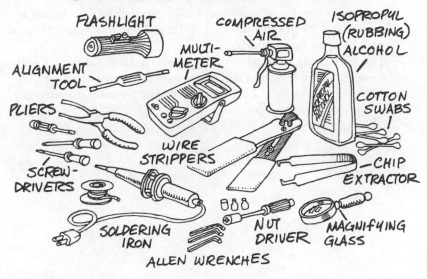

FLASHLIGHT   COMPRESSED   ISOPROPUL
                   AIR   (RUBBING)
                              ALCOHOL

ALIGNMENT   MULTI-
   TOOL   METER

PLIERS   COTTON
                              SWABS

             WIRE
SCREW-   STRIPPERS
DRIVERS   CHIP
                              EXTRACTOR

SOLDERING   NUT   MAGNIFYING
  IRON   DRIVER GLASS

ALLEN WRENCHES

Special Tools. There are two very useful and inexpensive tools that you should be able to find at a local electronics supply store, such as Radio Shack. The first is an alignment tool—basically, a plastic screwdriver. The second is a tweezerlike chip-extraction tool. There's also an L-shaped chip-extraction tool, which prys a chip loose. These cost less than a dollar or two apiece and will come in handy at times, although you can get by without them. If you plan to do soldering (you don't need to do much or any for most of the repairs in this book), you'll need to invest in a soldering iron, preferably a "pencil-type" iron. The iron should be in the 20-to-40 watt range.

Other Tools. You can easily spend $500 to $1,500 on a standard electronics tool kit, but you'll basically get just more of the above, complete with a genuine leather carrying case. Other handy items, some of which you probably already have around the house, include a mirror (preferably one with a long, skinny handle, like dentists use), a flashlight, tweezers, and a magnifying glass. If you want to be really well equipped, additional tools to consider are a wire cutter/stripper, a set of allen wrenches, and a desoldering tool. You probably should hold off getting these last three items until you actually need them, however.

One more tip: Keep your tool kit, or as much of it as possible, in one place, preferably in a small box. That way you'll always have what you need handy.

The nice thing about Everybody's Fix-It Tool Kit is that with few exceptions every item will prove useful for other home repair tasks, so you needn't shell out big bucks on tools to save big bucks on computer repairs.

PART II

FIX IT

4
CENTRAL PROCESSORS

At its most basic level, a computer consists of a central processor and a variety of peripheral devices, such as a monitor, keyboard, printer, and modem. The central processor, at the heart of it all, has a rather significant mission: to process words and data and to control all the activities of the computer. It may seem that much of what follows is too technical or otherwise inappropriate for a book on computer repairs. (If you're not technically inclined, you may want to skip directly to Signs of Trouble in this chapter, page 50.) But with the system overview contained in this chapter it will be considerably easier to get a handle on how your computer works and what is wrong with it when it doesn't.

At the heart of every central processor is a microprocessor— the brains of the computer. Among the more popular microprocessors in the world of personal computing are Intel Corporation's 8080, 8088, 8086, 80186, and 80286; Zilog's Z80, Z80A, and Z80B; Motorola's 6800 and 68010; and the MOS Technology 6502. If you have a personal computer, chances are you have one of these chips or one of their later versions, which have similar, but updated, numbers.

In a supporting role to the microprocessor is a computer's memory. Some of it is permanent memory (read-only memory, or ROM); the rest is temporary memory (random-access memory, or RAM).

Finally, there are a number of specialized circuits and discrete integrated-circuit chips. These include various circuits that link the central processor to its "outside world" of printers, modems, and other components. Other circuits control disk drives and provide the smarts to keep data streaming out to the computer's screen. A central processor also may include various other circuits to do such things as keep track of the time and date.

Big Boards and Slots

Personal computers come in two basic varieties: single-board machines and multiboard machines containing a "motherboard" (also known as a "backplane"), a principal circuit board into which a number of other boards may be plugged. Among the former are computers made by Radio Shack (the TRS-80 series), Kaypro, Atari, Commodore, and Texas Instruments. (Not all computers made by these companies are single-board types.) Those taking the multiboard approach include machines made by Apple and IBM, including the IBM PC and IBM compatibles.

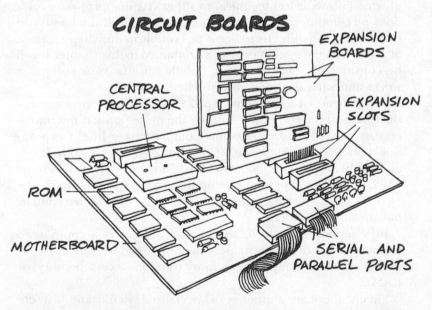

CIRCUIT BOARDS

EXPANSION BOARDS

CENTRAL PROCESSOR

EXPANSION SLOTS

ROM

MOTHERBOARD

SERIAL AND PARALLEL PORTS

The only difference that's important here is where components are located. On the single-board machines, you'll find the microprocessor, memory chips, and interface circuits all on one board. With a multiboard computer, you may find some or all circuits on a single board, with the extra plug-in boards providing additional memory, communication ports, or special functions, such as a clock/calendar circuit or print spooler. There are a number of computers on the market in which the motherboard is simply a space for plugging in other boards. The microprocessor, memory, and various interface circuits are all located on separate boards; the motherboard simply serves as a communication channel for connecting these separate boards.

Putting It All Together

Whether the various central processor circuits are on one board or on several doesn't matter when it comes to how these components work together. The main difference, from your perspective, is how much flexibility you have to tailor your computer to your particular needs. The more "slots" you have for extra boards, the more memory and other features you can add. Given the inventiveness of the computer industry, however, even this isn't entirely true: There are a number of products designed to be piggybacked onto a single-board computer.

There are a number of ways of looking at how a computer's central processor works. One useful way is to look at the sequence of events in the typical day of a computer, rather than looking at the individual components.

When you first turn on your computer, the microprocessor takes charge. Its very first step is to go to a specific location in memory (ROM) where it can obtain instructions on what to do next. It does this by sending out a signal indicating that it is going to take control of the "data bus"—a series of data lines on which information is transmitted among the various circuits of the central processor. It then sends out the address in memory from which it wants information on the "address bus"—a similar set of lines on which locations within memory (addresses) are communicated. The information is then transferred to the microprocessor, byte by byte. The first instructions the microprocessor gets may be simply to read a command file from a floppy disk and execute it. Or it may be a more complex sequence of commands designed to test various components of the computer as well as to

When Is a Reset a Reset?

You'll often encounter situations where, through your own mistake, a program bug, or a hardware malfunction, you must reset a computer to get things straight. You no doubt have found that there are a number of ways to "reset" your system and have probably discovered that some work sometimes but not always. Understanding how different reset levels affect a computer may aid you in figuring out whether a particular problem is related to hardware or to software.

Generically, there are two kinds of system resets. The first is frequently known as a "cold boot." Here you start from scratch. The power is turned off, then back on. This clears any problem conditions that resulted from a software error and under certain circumstances can clear some hardware problems, although not hardware defects. It is possible to do the equivalent of a cold boot in software simply by exiting from the program to the operating system, transferring control to the operating system sequence your machine goes through when you turn it on.

Whether you can do a cold boot in software depends on

check how the computer is configured—how much memory it has, the number of disk drives connected, whether there's a printer, and so on. This is known as a "self-test."

After completing the initial sequence—known in computer jargon as "booting"—the computer may display a prompt and await your command, or it may be set up to automatically load a specific program. To get a program from your disk into memory, the microprocessor sends a series of instructions to the disk controller. These instructions are part of the operating system program.

what kind of problem you are dealing with when you attempt it. Whichever way you do a cold boot—turning the power off or going through software—the computer will go through all the steps it normally does when you first turn it on.

A word of caution here. There are times when an error may have locked up some electrical component by switching various logic circuits to a pattern that leaves the system totally confused. Normally, shutting the power off is all it takes to have everything pop back to its initial state. But it may take a little time to do this—thirty seconds or more. Various components are designed to store an electrical charge; others do so even though they weren't designed for this purpose. It takes a little time to "bleed" the accumulated electricity out of these circuits, and this may account for things not coming back to normal even though you turned the machine off.

The second level of reset is known as a "warm boot." It can be done by pushing a reset button on some systems or by hitting a special keyboard key or sequence, such as "CTRL-BREAK" or "CTRL-C." This leaves the computer on but moves control to a portion of the operating system just beyond where the initial start-up sequence is located.

Like a cold boot, a warm boot simply transfers control from wherever you happen to be when the system crashed to some more basic initial sequence. Typically, you won't see any kind of real activity on a warm boot; the system will simply display the familiar operating system prompt.

Talking to a Disk

The first set of instructions that go to the disk controller requests it to set up the disk drive to read the disk's directory to find the location of the program on the disk. The operating system program knows the precise location of the directory, so the actual instructions to the controller are to go to that location and transfer the information there into the computer's memory. Examined closely, what happens is that a series of program instructions in the operating system program are transferred to the microprocessor, which, in turn, executes those instructions. Among the instructions are ones to transfer specific information from the disk, through the disk controller, along the data bus, and into a designated location in memory.

Once everything is set up, the microprocessor begins sending a series of instructions to the controller that tells it to begin transferring information from the disk. As each byte is read into the controller, the controller sets a flag letting the microprocessor know that a byte is ready for transfer to memory. Depending on the type of file being transferred, the microprocessor either "knows" how much information it will be transferring or it examines each character until it sees one that indicates the end of the file has been reached. (In some computers the microprocessor finds the length of a file from the disk directory, which enables it to set up a counter to read that much information.)

Some computers are designed with special circuits (known as "direct-memory access," or DMA), which take some of the burden off the microprocessor when it comes to zipping information around the computer. As described above, each step in the processor is under the direct control of the microprocessor. With a DMA system, the microprocessor merely sets things up and then is free to perform certain other operations while the transfer is completed.

Assume for a moment that a word processing program is transferred into memory. Once the transfer is complete, the operating system program partially releases control of the computer to the word processing program. It knows from the disk directory, or the file itself, that what it has transferred is a program file. Knowing that, its last instruction to the microprocessor is to begin reading in the program's instructions. As it does this, the microprocessor begins to tell the various parts of the computer to do whatever the word processing program wants done.

One of the first things the word processing program does is to get a picture of what's going on in memory. Typically, the lower part of memory is where the program itself resides. The operating system generally sits in the top part of memory. (Memory locations are numbered, beginning at location 0000—the "bottom"—and going up to whatever the upper limit is in a particular system.)

To find out what's going on in memory, the operating system reads a specific location in the central processor that tells it how much memory is available for its use and where that memory is located. It may also check to see whether or not there is a printer hooked up and ready to go or whether you have a black-and-white or a color display. So far, the whole process has taken maybe a few seconds.

Pictures of a Thousand Words

Next comes a set of instructions to set up your display. The microprocessor transfers the information to be displayed from the program to a portion of memory set aside for the display. This part of memory represents a matrix of the rows and columns of your screen. A cycle is set up to transfer the information in a fixed sequence from memory to the screen over and over, dozens of times a second, to keep the screen image "refreshed." As is the case with transferring information from disk to memory, this may be done directly by the microprocessor or independent of the microprocessor—by special circuitry.

As soon as all this is set up and going smoothly, the word processing program sends a new set of instructions to the microprocessor telling it to check the keyboard for new information. The program is looking for you to issue a command or to start typing text. Let's assume the first character it needs is one that tells it how you want your screen set up—things like left and right margins, tabs, and so on. The screen's cursor key flashes on and off as a "prompt," indicating it wants some action from you.

Let's stop for a minute and take a look at the keyboard. It is hooked up to a circuit very similar to a floppy disk controller. When a character comes into the keyboard controller, the controller raises a flag to let the microprocessor know it has a character. The microprocessor then "reads" the character from the keyboard interface and either brings it directly into one of its data registers or puts it somewhere in memory, depending on what the program's creators instructed it to do.

A microprocessor register is much like a memory cell. In fact, all microprocessors have several memory cells as well as special registers for storing and interpreting program instructions and finding in memory the location of the next instruction. In most cases, once a character is in a register, it runs through the microprocessor's arithmetic/logic unit, where it is added, subtracted, multiplied, divided, compared with another character in another register, or otherwise subjected to one or more logical operations.

Let's get back to the word processing example at hand. Once the microprocessor is notified by the keyboard interface that a character is available, and the microprocessor has brought the character into memory, the program typically compares it with another character (or set of characters) to determine just what it is you want to do. A comparison tells the program whether a particular character is equal to, less than, or greater than some other character. This permits the computer to know what it is going to do next through a test instruction that says if such and such is true, then go do this, that, or the other thing. If it isn't true, then do something else. To "do something else," the microprocessor goes to another location in memory for additional instructions.

Let's say the next instruction is to wait for you to type in text. As you do, the microprocessor checks the keyboard interface for characters. As your fingers zip lightning-fast across the keys, cranking out the next Pulitzer nominee, the microprocessor sends each character to a place in memory for storage as well as to the display storage and interface so it can be shown to you on your screen. As you well know, all this happens instantaneously, more or less.

The program probably reviews every character you type to determine whether it is text or a sequence it interprets as something else, such as a command to delete the previous character, move the cursor, store a document, or perform some other word processing function.

So, as you sit there being literary, your computer is working diligently, checking the keyboard interface for characters, send-

Board Swapping

If you bring your circuit board to your favorite computer store for a quickie repair—say, resoldering a loose chip— what you get back may not necessarily be what you brought in.

If this were your car and your neighborhood garage, you'd know the minute you picked up the car that a defective part had been replaced rather than had had a five-minute repair done to it. You'd have a hefty bill and might even have an oily old part sitting on the seat next to you.

Computer stores and repair centers won't jar you like this, but they also may not tell you that the board you walked in with is now sitting on their shelf, waiting for a lull in the repair business before the technician heats up a soldering iron to fix it.

This is neither a problem nor bad business practice. Due to the typical arrangements stores and repair centers have with manufacturers and distributors, it doesn't cost them anything to swap a board and charge you as though they had fixed your original one. You probably come out ahead, too. Your machine is up and running in minutes rather than the days it might take for a technician to make the necessary repair. And the cost is the same, or at least approximately so.

Still, it pays to find out if the store has switched boards on you. If you got a new board in the deal, you should burn it in, or you may run the risk of failure. If the board is new, it should come with a warranty, and you should receive a copy. And if your board had a number of built-in features— serial or parallel ports, a clock/calendar, a print spooler, or a RAM disk, for example—the replacement board should be comparably equipped.

ing them madly out to the screen, and tending to a number of other tasks necessary to keep its house in order. Among those housekeeping tasks are such things as rewriting everything to memory several times a second so it stays in memory.

A Trip Down Memory Lane

So far we've discussed two types of memory—RAM and ROM. RAM is temporary memory available for your programs and data. When you turn your machine off, you lose whatever information was stored in RAM. ROM, on the other hand, retains what's stored in it even after the computer is turned off, much like you retain the information on a phonograph record when you turn off your stereo. (The real differences between RAM and ROM aren't very well expressed in their names. While it is true that you can't write anything into ROM—it is truly "read-only"—it can be accessed randomly, just like RAM.)

There are many kinds of computer chips. Two chips described as "RAM" or "ROM" may be very different from each other. Among RAM chips the two major differences are between those known as "static RAM," which retain information until the power is turned off or new information is written in the same location, and "dynamic RAM," which retains information only for a small fraction of a second unless it is rewritten by the computer. Most personal computers use dynamic RAM because it is much cheaper than static RAM. The rewriting of RAM is done under the general direction of the microprocessor. You may be merely sitting there—staring at your screen, looking for an appropriate adverb—but in the background your computer is humming away, refreshing its memory.

A Paper World

At some point, you finish writing and tell your program you want to store your literary masterminding on a disk, where it will be safe and relatively permanent. You may also want a printed copy. So you ask the program to zip a copy off to your printer.

First, let's store the document on a disk. With the appropriate commands, the program sends off instructions to write information to a disk. This is essentially the reverse of the reading process. The information is transferred from memory to the disk controller and then sent to the disk. As each character is written onto the disk, the controller sends up a flag indicating it is ready for the next character. This goes on until all information is transferred. When that is done, the disk directory is brought up to date.

Now it's time to print. To do this (after you've given the magic command), the microprocessor goes to the interface circuitry to which your printer is linked. It then checks to see whether the printer is ready to accept anything. If everything is ready, the microprocessor begins transferring characters from memory to the printer interface and then to the printer.

A lot of what is known as "handshaking" goes on here. The microprocessor constantly checks to see if the printer is ready for another character; if it isn't, it tries to find out why.

At this point, we have come full circle. The program is probably asking the microprocessor to check to see if there is another character at the keyboard interface, which it can use to determine what to do next. You send off the command indicating you are tired of processing words and want to quit. The word processing program turns control back to the operating system's executive command sequence, which asks the microprocessor to keep checking the keyboard to see what you want to do next.

By the way, the operating system program hasn't been sitting by doing nothing all this time. Nearly everything your program does is really an instruction to a particular part of your operating system. Your instruction to the program may indicate "read something from the keyboard," but the program itself doesn't contain the detailed instructions necessary to do this. It more than likely passes the buck, sending your instruction someplace in the operating system for execution. Once this instruction is completed, the operating system tells the microprocessor to go back to your program for the next instruction.

There. Chances are you've just learned more about the workings of a microprocessor than the salesperson from whom you purchased your computer. Now let's take a look at what can go wrong and what you can do about it.

Signs of Trouble

As we've said before, electrical components are generally reliable. If you take your machine through an initial burn-in period (see Before the Warranty Runs Out, page 10), there is a good chance—barring equipment abuse and acts of God—that the components will outlast the useful life of your computer. This, of course, applies only to the electrical components.

This is not to say that you aren't going to have real problems. But, once again, most of the time you have a problem, it will be because a component—a circuit board or socketed integrated circuit—has worked itself loose or because its connection with the rest of the system has become contaminated with dirt and grime. When this happens, the solution is to unseat the board or component, clean the contacts, and reseat it. If it works, you're a repair genius.

Now for those times when the problem is serious.

Probably the biggest frustration in solving computer problems is that when they involve the central processor, problems tend to be erratic and symptoms often misleading.

Let's say you start running a program at nine in the morning. At eleven-thirty, the machine hangs up—you hit a key and nothing happens. An obvious conclusion is that there is something wrong with the keyboard—the computer isn't responding when you strike a key. But let's trace it through. Sure, it could be the keyboard, but it also could be any of the following:

* the cable connecting the keyboard to the rest of the computer
* the circuitry that links the keyboard to the central processor
* the portion of memory that tells the computer what should be displayed when you press a particular key
* the microprocessor, which continually checks the keyboard interface for a character

Zapping
Delicate Circuits

Most computer components are hardy enough to with-stand abuse. Other components, particularly those known as CMOS—complementary metal oxide semiconductors—are very delicate electronically and can be easily ruined with static electricity. When you start poking around inside your computer, especially if you plan to add memory chips to your system or to pull chips for whatever reason, you must take steps to prevent static from ruining the chips.

If there is noticeable static—if you see sparks flying every time you move around or touch a doorknob, for example—you should set up a humidifier to lessen the static. Don't mess with the computer until you have raised the humidity. Another precaution is to touch something metal in your com-puter before touching a chip or your system. The computer must be plugged in so that you have a true ground contact.

Then proceed cautiously. Touch one hand to your com-puter's chassis and keep it there while you poke around. This has the effect of keeping you and the machine at the same potential and should be all that is necessary to prevent sparks from flying around, zapping expensive chips.

* the part of memory that contains the section of your pro-gram that is asking for a character
* the part of the operating system program routine that tells the microprocessor to look for a character from the key-board interface

As you see, the source of the problem is anything but obvious. You can't do anything, so you hit the reset button and reload the program from the disk. Everything works fine. Now the computer once again accepts a character from your keyboard. Everything seems to be running fine. You punch a few more keys and quit for lunch. When you return an hour later, the machine won't respond to your keystrokes.

What's going on here?

Unfortunately, this is not atypical. And when it happens, it leaves you facing a large number of unanswered questions. The problem is that a computer is a collection of related parts. When something goes wrong, it could be anything in the entire system. Because you can't simply repair or replace everything in the system, you have to pin the problem down to the defective part. That's easier said than done, but it's not impossible.

Let's look more closely at this hypothetical but frequent problem of the computer not responding to the keyboard.

Trees for the Forest

The key to success is to separate a problem like this into its components and test each individually to see if it is the problem's cause. Let's review the elements that may be culprits:

* the keyboard
* the cable connecting the keyboard to the computer
* the interface circuitry that captures input from your keyboard
* the part of memory where instructions are kept to transform keyboard signals into recognizable characters on the screen
* the lines connecting the keyboard interface and the rest of the central processor
* the microprocessor
* the portion of memory where the program is located
* the portion of memory where the operating system keyboard routines are located

You now systematically test each of these until you locate the problem, right?

Wrong. You've just been led into a frustrating trap. Being systematic is very important and cannot be overstressed. But, by the same token, there is no need to tie yourself up in a web of details that may lead you away from the obvious answer to the problem.

What are the easy ways to find out what is wrong? Simply reload the program. If you can't reload it because the computer won't respond to your commands, then you have to start running through some of the steps above to find out what is wrong. If it does reload, then you haven't wasted time exploring all the possible causes.

If the program can be reloaded, you should ask yourself a few quick questions.

* Is there any obvious place in the program where it is locking up? (Does it happen only when trying to move a paragraph, for example, or when trying to store something?)
* Is there any obvious environmental condition that may be suspect? (Is the room hot? Has there just been a lightning storm?)
* Have I abused my computer in any way? (Consider spills, dust, cigarette smoke, bumping, and jarring.)
* Are strange things happening with the power? (Are the room lights flickering or dimming, for example?)

Answering these broader questions first will likely be far more fruitful than chasing down every possible detail. This isn't to say that you won't ultimately have to get to the heart of your problem, but start with the big stuff.

If you have successfully reloaded your program, you should try using it. If the program works, what probably happened was that some sort of temporary glitch zapped the section of memory where your program resided. When that happens, everything else simply goes to pieces. Program instructions make no sense to the microprocessor, so it just sits there until you hit the reset button.

If, on the other hand, the program continues to fail, look at some of the broader questions above. If none of these looks like a prime suspect, try running a similar program and see if things continue to crash. This way, you can implicate the original program if another program hums along. (*Note:* There are lots of programs on the market that contain bugs that will cause a program to go haywire under certain conditions—and you, of course, invoke these conditions without fail. But a program can sustain these types of errors after it's put on disk, so don't be too quick to blame the program's publisher. If you suspect the program, try loading a backup copy to see if it works.)

When testing in this manner, assume the program is going to crash and take appropriate precautions to protect whatever work you are doing, such as assuring that the program and data disks you are using have backup copies.

Let's take a quick look at the central processor as a whole and some of its specific components to see what kinds of things can go wrong.

What Can Go Wrong

Examine your central processor circuit board. What you see are a number of lines connecting integrated circuits and a few discrete components. You'll notice that most ICs are soldered into place, but a few—typically the more expensive ones and those subject to change, such as the ROM chips—are mounted in sockets that, in turn, are soldered to the board. The only thing that moves here are electrons, so there's nothing to wear out from friction.

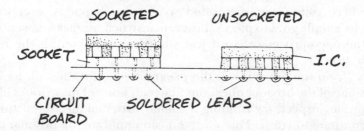

The differences among the various subsystems on the central processor board are irrelevant when it comes to troubleshooting. Certain types of components react differently to heat and to other types of abuse, but unless you are prepared to delve deeply into the realm of computer hardware, the differences won't matter in your effort to keep your computer healthy. If you're trying to get to the bottom of a problem, it won't really matter that you have memory chips, a microprocessor chip, and various parallel and serial interface chips and circuits. In most cases, you won't be dealing with them individually.

So, what can go wrong? Plenty.

* Defective components can break down as they are subject to heat.
* Undersoldered connections can fail, and oversoldered ones can short circuit.
* The circuit lines and traces on a board can get scratched or otherwise damaged, breaking a circuit.
* Dirt and dust can cause heat buildup and short circuits.
* Socketed chips or other plug-in circuit boards can be jarred loose by vibration of a fan or disk drive motor, or a socket connection can be broken by the buildup of dirt and dust.
* Contacts can oxidize.
* Power surges can burn a part out. Static electricity can have the same effect.

The accumulation of dirt, the loosening of socketed connections, the oxidation of contacts, and power surges are problems that can plague computers over the long term. Other problems are likely to show up early in a computer's life, particularly if you take it through a burn-in period. (See Before the Warranty Runs Out, page 10.) Assuming your machine works when you first put it together, the symptoms of any such problems will appear to be very similar. Some problems will show up only intermittently, then seem to "fix" themselves. Here are some of the biggest offenders.

Heat. When computer components heat up, they tend to fail. It may not be a permanent failure, although it can lead to one in the long run. In summer you may find your computer doing erratic things. Shutting it down for an hour or so "fixes" it. The same things can happen even on a cool day if there is a heat buildup inside your machine due to blocked ventilation ducts, a defective power supply, or just prolonged use in a stuffy room.

MEMORY CHIP

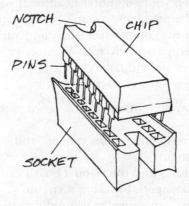

Heat problems are compounded if a component is weak to begin with, but even healthy components stop functioning properly when overheated. Heat causes expansion. Inside a tiny IC, that can mean a short circuit as two tiny circuits expand into each other, or it can simply expand a circuit beyond its limit, breaking continuity.

Heat problems will be aggravated if your computer is dirty. The accumulated filth tends to trap heat, making a marginal problem a major one.

Dirt and Smoke. Dirt, dust, and cigarette smoke have no place in a computer. It's bad enough that you insist upon damaging your health with cigarettes, but your computer doesn't need that kind of abuse. While it's no longer necessary to keep a computer in a specially treated, smoke-free room, smoke and dirt will cause a computer to break down. In most cases, the damage will be temporary; occasionally, it may be fatal.

Dirt and smoke contribute to machine failure in two ways. First, it's possible for enough filth and grime to accumulate to cause two circuits to come into contact with each other. Second, if you have enough gunk, you can block the flow of electrons in a circuit —particularly where you have socketed ICs or additional circuit boards plugged into the motherboard.

Defective Components. If you were good in your previous lives, your computer's manufacturer will have caught all weak components in your computer before it passed inspection. The rest of us are likely at one time or another to be victims of the statistical quirks of quality control systems, which catch every bad product except the one intended for us.

Follow the advice about burning your machine in and, if you are one of those upon whom luck rarely smiles, at least it won't cost you anything to get your machine fixed while it's under warranty. By the way, whenever you get the machine back from the repair shop, burn in any replaced parts.

Defective components are clever little beasts. They may chug along until you are really doing something important on your machine. Then they'll fail, probably only temporarily. They even have a way of foisting blame for a problem off onto another chip or even onto a different area of the computer altogether. One time they'll make a program stop working. The next time they'll put mysterious but aggravating garbage on a disk. Then they'll zap part of your screen or make it appear that your keyboard has gone awry.

If you are up to it, obtain circuit and block diagrams for your computer. With their aid you can find your way around a circuit board and nail a bad chip. But unless you're an electrical engineer or technician, it's a lot of trouble and probably not the purpose for which you bought a computer. If you're the type who likes to play with assembly language programs and you have become really hooked on hacking, by all means get the block diagrams. You'll learn a lot about how your machine works—the wonders of digital logic—and should have no problem when it comes to troubleshooting a bad circuit or chip.

Everyone else should leave the search for defective parts to the pros.

Bad Soldering. Another problem comes from bad soldering. This isn't a human error; most soldering on your computer is done on an automated assembly line.

One common problem is stray solder. Sometimes a little bit of solder ends up somewhere it doesn't belong, connecting two circuit lines or shorting two pins on a chip. This happens despite

GOOD AND BAD
SOLDER CONNECTIONS

NOT   JUST   TOO
ENOUGH   RIGHT   MUCH

the fact that manufacturers go to a lot of trouble to avoid this. Still, some bad boards slip through.

One reason they can slip through is that bad soldering doesn't always result in a bad connection, so a poorly soldered board may go undetected when checked out. Even after you plug it into your computer, it may still not foul things up—initially, at least. Over time, however, it may affect the operation of your machine intermittently.

A particularly troublesome solder problem is the stray little ball of solder that rolls around, shorting one place for a while, rolling around some more and shorting something else. These electrical whirling dervishes can cause very different problems depending on where they decide to settle, making them nerve-wracking, to say the least.

Equally subtle but a bit easier to pin down are undersoldered connections. What happens here is that the solder is in place— just enough to pass testing and visual inspection—but the connection is bad. Eventually, it will come loose.

Potholes on Your Computer's Highways

Linking all the components on a circuit board are a number of etched lines and traces (which look like tinfoil strips). Many are very, very thin and are easily scratched, which breaks electrical continuity. Moreover, the underlying circuit board can be damaged or cracked; any flexing causes a break in a circuit located above a damaged area.

Typically, if you do the scratching, you'll know you've done it and can see the damage. If the scratch originated elsewhere, it won't necessarily be obvious, especially if it results from a manufacturing defect. These more subtle defects are often difficult to find because they may not be visible—after all, the lines are only a few millimeters wide. Naturally, they tend to cause sporadic, rather than total, failures.

Socket to 'Em

Socketed ICs and plug-in circuit boards have a way of vibrating themselves loose. They also can be great repositories of filth and goop. After a while, pulling boards and chips and reseating them can wear the contacts out, although you'd really have to be a maniac to do this often enough to have much effect.

Little more need be said about this. Pulling a chip or plug-in board and reseating it is one of those wondrous repairs that regularly remedy a wide range of hardware sins. *Never* pull a chip or board with the power on. But pulling chips is something anyone can do without doing time at MIT. You remove both a board and a chip the same way: Rock the board or chip gently back and forth as you pull. Don't force anything. When inserting, push evenly while rocking the board gently. Use both hands on a plug-in board to provide even pressure along the length of the board. (See illustration page 60.)

Sparks Are Flying

As a kid, you no doubt charged yourself up during the winter by rubbing your sweater until you built up what seemed like several million volts, then zapped your unsuspecting little sister or best friend on the nose. Like your little sister, many integrated circuits are very, very sensitive and can be zapped simply by your sitting down at your computer on a dry winter day, to say nothing of the static damage you can do if you actually poke around inside the thing.

The Soviets may be missing a golden opportunity to depict the

INSERTING AN EXPANSION BOARD

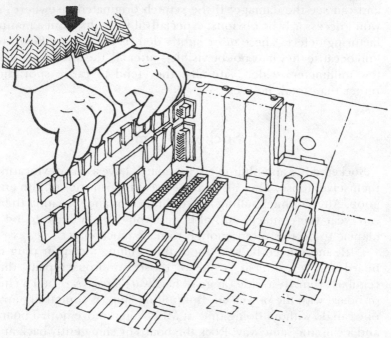

enslavement of American workers. If they were to visit a factory where delicate ICs are assembled onto working circuit boards, they'd see workers wearing metal bracelets with wires dangling off them, attached to ground. The purpose of connecting workers to the ground isn't to fatten some capitalist's bank account but to try to control static electricity that would otherwise put the capitalist in debtors' prison, as IC after IC gets ruined by human-generated static electricity.

If you find your computer doing erratic things on a cold, dry winter day, chances are high that static electricity is at work. When the atmosphere is dry, it's a good idea to find some big metal cabinet or other object on which to unload your static charge; simply touch it before touching your computer. When you are about to touch something inside the computer, always touch the chassis first. *(Note:* Touching the chassis helps only if your computer is plugged in.)

HOW TO CONTROL STATIC ELECTRICITY

One final problem is oxidation. This doesn't occur often—most materials used in your computer have a rather high oxidation threshold—but it does happen. If you live near water or have been foolish enough to stick your computer in a damp, dank room, you are a candidate for oxidation problems, particularly where two components plug together.

What You Can and Can't Do

There is almost nothing on the central processor board you can't fix, especially if you are adept with a solder gun. The problem is that you can't fix something if you don't know what's broken, and finding out what needs mending can be a bit tricky.

As the discussion above should make clear, most of the time you think you have a hardware problem, something else—operator error or bad programming—is at fault. You also may have some other external problem, like flaky power, excessive heat, or plain old static electricity causing your computer to fail. If some-

Adding
Additional Memory

Many of us bought computers with the minimum amount of memory we could buy and still have the salesperson let us out the door. And many of us later realized that more is better—at least more than 64K. Your computer may have sockets on its main circuit board (or motherboard) for additional random-access memory (RAM). If so, expansion is easy—it's nothing more than popping a few memory chips into the sockets and setting a switch or two to let your computer know you've rewarded it with greater memory capacity.

Unless you've added an expansion board that contains its own memory slots, you must add the same-size memory chips that already exist in your computer. That is, if your computer contains 1K memory chips, you must add 1K chips. Ditto for 16K, 64K, and 256K chips. Moreover, they must operate at the same access speed as the existing chips. Finally, chips must usually be added in sets of eight or nine.

Finding out what you need is pretty straightforward. You can open your computer and get the chip number off the existing memory chips. You should be a little careful here because most chips are available from several firms and may not contain the same generic chip number; instead, they'll have a manufacturer's number. That shouldn't be a problem. When you purchase your chips, simply provide whatever number you have.

There isn't a big price spread on memory chips, so you might as well buy from a local computer store or electronics supply house. This will make it a bit easier to get replacements if a chip turns out to be bad—a fairly common occurrence.

You may also be able to get memory chips at a savings through a users' group, a local computer club, or a computer bulletin board. If you are looking for 16K or even 64K chips, you may find these available from computer owners who have switched to larger-size units.

Installing the chips is duck soup, but take care. First, turn the power off. Static is a definite no-no, and you should follow the steps outlined in Zapping Delicate Circuits (page 51) as far as grounding yourself to your machine.

The chips must go in their sockets correctly. You can determine the correct alignment by examining existing chips and making sure you align the new ones in the same way. One end of the chip has a notch that will either match or be the reverse of a similar notch in the socket.

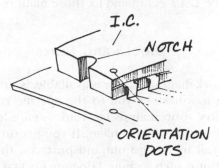

CHIP NOTCH

I.C.

NOTCH

ORIENTATION DOTS

You can use a tweezerlike chip puller to insert the chips in their sockets, but it is just as easy to use your hands. It should require a bit of pressure to seat the chips completely, but not so much that you bend or break its leg. Gently insert the chip in the socket, making sure all the legs are going in properly. Then use a little more pressure. Rock the chip into place, pushing one end down a little, then the other.

Make sure they're in all the way. Look at existing chips, and try to get the new ones to seat as far down as the older ones. Don't worry about fractions of an inch, especially if you find the resistance so great that you risk breaking a leg on the chip. "Close" counts in horseshoes and seating chips.

What happens if you bend a leg? They can be straightened if you are careful—use your fingers, not a tool. If the bend is really a break or if straightening the leg causes a fracture, you'll be better off tossing the chip. Otherwise you'll risk having a bad chip, either now or in the near future.

Pleasant memories.

thing has gone wrong inside your machine, fixing it may involve little more than cleaning a circuit board or reseating a board or socketed chip.

Having failed from all this, however, it's time to get down to the nitty-gritty. Let's get in and fix those malfunctioning boards.

Blocks and Lines

A circuit block diagram, if one is available, is a useful diagnostic tool because it will steer you to the specific components and related circuitry your analysis has told you are likely candidates for being the source of a problem. If you get turned on by such diagrams, by all means go out and purchase them—they are a definite aid. But if such technical documents make you break out in a cold sweat, don't despair, they aren't all that necessary.

Even without circuit diagrams, you probably can find your way around a circuit board. The microprocessor tends to be a big chip, and the board itself might even be marked "CPU" or "MPU." More likely, the CPU is marked with its model number: Z80, 8088, 68000, 6502, or the like.

Directly associated with the microprocessor, although not necessarily located near it, is what is known as a clock circuit. This part of the board keeps every other component marching to the beat of the same drummer. It has a few ICs, one of which is an oscillator (a crystal just like the one in your digital watch that beats out a pulse) and a few other chips that take this signal and

CIRCUIT BOARD COMPONENTS

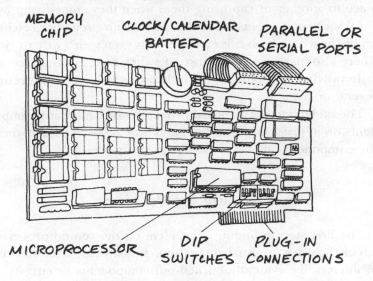

MEMORY CHIP   CLOCK/CALENDAR BATTERY   PARALLEL OR SERIAL PORTS

MICROPROCESSOR   DIP SWITCHES   PLUG-IN CONNECTIONS

modify the beat for different circuits. You may find more than one clock circuit if your monitor requires a separate clock and even one that gives you the time and date.

You probably can't miss the RAM memory chips because they tend to come in banks of eight or nine, all in nice little rows. ROM chips may be spread all over the place—some are as big as the microprocessor, others are tiny things. They tend to wear little paper labels saying things like "A," "B," and "C," or "REV D.1." Some ROM chips may be associated with the keyboard and video interfaces, among other components.

Around the edge of the main board, you'll find connectors to the printer, modem, keyboard, joystick, monitor, and who knows what else. Associated with each may be a number of little ICs, but in most cases there will be at least one big one. Chances are it will be marked "SIO" or "PIO," for serial and parallel input-output, respectively.

Somewhere on the board you may find a floppy disk controller, video drivers, power-regulation chips, and other things. There will be lots of transistors, diodes, resistors, capacitors, and tiny little ICs that serve vital functions, such as shoving data from one place to another or capturing them when they come flying by.

All such components are tied together with circuit lines etched on the board on both sides and perhaps even with a wire or two. There also may be a row or two of switch boxes with five or six little switches and some similar little boxes with wires connecting several points.

The underside of the board probably won't have any components on it, just a bunch of lines and little blobs of solder where the components above are soldered into place.

Finding the Problem

The first step in finding a problem on the central processor circuit board is a visual inspection. Initially, look for obvious problems, like evidently burned-out components or circuits. If they are there, you won't have much trouble spotting them. An IC may swell up, resistors and capacitors can quite literally blow up, and other components may generate enough heat to leave a telltale burned area on the board.

Next, look for subtle problems, like the accumulation of dirt and dust, bad solder connections (particularly on the underside), and broken circuit lines. Also look for obvious loose connections, components, or stray material. If you can remove the entire board with ease, give it a shake or two and see if anything rattles.

If your computer has a motherboard and a number of independent boards, you should go ahead and loosen and reseat each. Never mind that they look as if they're already in place—pull them out, then stick them back in.

As long as you have them out, go ahead and inspect the connections (at least the male side; the female side may be difficult to see). If the connections look dirty, you have a couple of choices. You can clean them with a bit of isopropyl (rubbing) alcohol, or you can do the old eraser trick. Get a clean eraser and gently rub the surface of the connection. Take it easy—the idea is to merely clean it up, not remove the coating. Be careful not to gum things up with bits of eraser.

If your computer has a dampness problem, due either to working in a basement or to living near water, you might want to invest in a can of electrical-contact/relay cleaner. This will cost about $3.00 or $4.00 for a can that will last a lifetime. Good old WD-40 and related products are pretty popular and a bit cheaper. Given the small quantities you'll use, the difference in cost hardly matters. Moderation, no matter which cleaner you use, is advised.

Use the cleaner on any connection or switch, taking care to use the least amount you can get away with. Don't spray so much that it runs off—a little dab'll do ya.

Pulling Chips

Next come the socketed ICs. You may simply have to push them gently to make sure they are firmly in place, or you may find it necessary to pull each one out to clean the contacts if you suspect dirt buildup. You also should blast the connections with canned air or your trusty vacuum cleaner running in reverse.

When you pull ICs, do it one at a time so you don't make mistakes about what goes where. Make a drawing, map, or list of what chip goes in what socket—and in what position—so each can go back from where it came. This is really important. If you put an IC in backward or in the wrong slot, you'll wreak havoc on the logical functions it's supposed to perform. You may well harm it and other chips electrically. Fortunately, manufacturers have thought about folks like you, so in most cases you'll find that a socketed chip has a notch at one end that matches a notch on the socket itself. *Beware: Not all socketed chips have notches, and sometimes the correct position has the notches reversed.* Write the correct orientation down before you pull the chip. If there is nothing on the chip to determine one end from the other, mark one end of both the chip and the socket with a felt tip or a piece of tape.

The earlier warnings we made about static electricity are very important when you actually handle the chips. Touch something

PULLING A CHIP

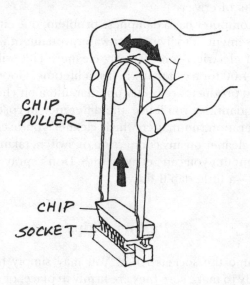

CHIP
PULLER

CHIP
SOCKET

metal (away from the computer) to discharge your static electricity. Then ground yourself to the machine by touching something metal that's harmless, like the chassis. The machine must be plugged in to get a true ground contact.

You're best-off using a plastic alignment tool to remove a chip, although you can use a small screwdriver. You can buy a socket-pulling tool for a few bucks at an electrical supply store, but it isn't really necessary. Pry one end of the socket up, then pry a little on the other end. Be gentle. The idea is to free the IC but not break or bend any of its legs. Don't use an eraser on the legs; they're too delicate. If the legs appear corroded, use contact cleaner or alcohol to clean them.

A Hot Touch

If visual inspection doesn't find your problem and pulling and reseating boards and ICs doesn't help either, the next step is the hot-and-cold approach. It really helps at this stage to have zeroed in logically on which circuits may be causing you problems.

Generally, the ICs on a circuit board shouldn't be too hot. Nor should they be bone-chillingly cold. You may be able to find a bad IC by revving the computer up and letting it run for an hour or so, then shutting it off. Now *disconnect the power cord* and feel around. A really hot IC—one that burns your finger—is a dead IC. Similarly, one that is completely cold isn't passing any juice and is a candidate for the junkyard.

This is all relative, of course. Some chips will be a little warmer than others. How hot is "too hot" or how cold is "too cold" really depends on the chip and how it feels relative to the others.

If you think you have a bum chip, test your theory with a blast of "canned cold" or even an ice cube. Cooling a defunct chip won't fix it, but if the problem is intermittent you may be able to locate the bad chip this way. What you must do is to get things warm enough to cause your problem to appear. You can speed this up with a hair dryer, which will have the added advantage of blowing away dust.

The idea is to heat things up enough so that a weak chip will behave erratically. Any chip will go bad if it gets too hot, so you must be careful with this approach. Concentrate your heat in the area of the suspect chip, and do whatever it takes to get the problem to recur. Obviously, you must have the power on to do this, so be careful. Stay away from the power supply and, if your computer has a built-in CRT, be extra careful about getting near it, let alone touching it.

Now for the cold treatment. If you can get the problem going by heating things up, try cooling your suspected bad chip a bit to see if it clears the problem. You can buy "canned cold" in the form of freon under pressure at most electrical supply stores, but you can get by with a cheaper approach if you are very careful. Put an ice cube in a plastic sandwich bag that can be sealed *completely.* You don't want to drip water all over your computer's innards.

If it is really humid, be sure you don't drip condensation from the outside of the bag. You'll find it convenient to wrap the whole mess in a bit of cloth. Now, with the machine still running, put this against the suspected bad IC and see if your problem goes away. You want to cool things down, but be careful. Too much coolness can be as stressful as too much heat. Hold the ice cube against the IC for about thirty seconds to a minute. If that doesn't solve the problem, cooling it any more won't help either. Anyway, if it's a good chip, you might damage it if you go too far.

You May Never Know

If all of this is inconclusive, you may have to give up your sleuthing. You can run through the procedure one more time to see if any other hot-running chip can be cooled into correcting whatever problem you're having. Eventually, though, you may have to admit defeat and cart your machine off for repair.

If you are comfortable with circuit diagrams, put your trusty multimeter to work searching for a short circuit (use the ohmmeter setting), or, if you have access to details of a particular chip, check the voltage level at the appropriate pins.

With an ohmmeter, an open circuit will give you infinite resistance, while a short circuit will read "0." But all of this will be for naught unless you can find the appropriate circuits on a diagram or on the chip manufacturer's spec sheet. This level of troubleshooting is beyond the scope of this book.

Final Word

Let's make it perfectly clear: All of this can be quite frustrating and may lead you nowhere. Like any undertaking, your level of expertise and access to the right tools can make a world of difference in the degree of success you experience. Don't be discouraged. In most cases you'll come out ahead simply by trying.

If you systematically attack the problem and keep records of what you do, even if you run up against a dead end, you'll gain valuable insight into your computer and will start off just a little better prepared the next time you open it up to find out what's going wrong.

The repair technician, armed to the teeth with training and repair and diagnostic tools, also must admit defeat sometimes or at least move on to something more productive. You should, too.

5
DISK DRIVES

A floppy disk drive is a relatively simple device. It consists of two motors, one that turns a spindle to rotate a disk and a second that moves an arm containing one or two read/write heads to the desired position on a disk. Other components include various detectors, such as a light-emitting diode and photodetector combination, which help the drive find its place on the disk, and similar setups that let a computer know if a disk is write-protected or whether a disk drive door is open or closed.

The rest of the components provide support for these devices and assist in transferring data between a disk and the computer's central processor, through the wires leading from the central processor and one or more drive-control circuit boards. A disk drive's real smarts, however, usually are found on a separate disk-controller circuit, which provides the link between the central processor and the drive.

A disk drive, being mechanical, is one of the weakest points in your computer system. Anything that moves can wear out, and the rather precise alignments required to correctly read and write data from a disk eventually go out of whack. Moreover, a disk drive is exposed to all sorts of abuse as you cram disks in and yank them out. And a disk drive is exposed to a wide variety of environmental contaminants ranging from dust, dirt, and grime to cigarette smoke and an odd assortment of goop and gunk that travels into the device on the backs of floppy disks.

How They Work

A disk drive reads and writes data to and from a floppy disk much like you record or play back music on a tape recorder. With the disk drive motor spinning your disk (much like a turntable spins a record), a ceramic head (two heads, if you have a double-sided disk drive) is instructed by the computer to move in or out to a certain track, find a particular sector, and read or write data there. (Tracks may be thought of as being like the grooves on a record, although a floppy's tracks are electronic rather than physical grooves; sectors are subdivisions of a track.) Typically, there are either 48 or 96 tracks per inch on a floppy disk, although there are oddball systems with other track densities. The number of sectors and the number of bytes per sector vary widely from computer to computer.

ANATOMY OF A DISK

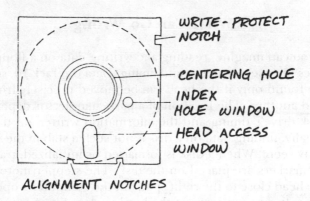

Data are stored on a disk one sector at a time. (When you copy a disk or perform certain other operations, a group of sectors—a "cluster"—or an entire track may be read or written at once.) The disk drive determines where a sector is located by referring to one or more small index holes in the floppy.

Disks that have just one such hole are called "soft-sectored" because they contain no built-in sectors; the computer electronically designates the sectors when you format or initialize the disk; disks with 10 or 16 holes are called "hard-sectored" disks, with sectors defined by the holes. If you're not sure which disk you use, just turn the disk to see whether you have one or more holes showing through the index hole.

A disk drive typically rotates 360 times a minute. Built into your operating system is software that adjusts for the difference in length of a disk drive's innermost and outermost tracks. The Apple Macintosh and some other computers using microdiskettes (3" disks) cram so much information into such a small space that they use far more sophisticated timing techniques on a track-by-track basis. With 48 tracks per inch (tpi), a disk drive stepper motor typically moves the head in and out in increments of $1/48"$ or less. A 96-tpi disk drive uses head movements of $1/96"$.

A read/write head is in direct contact with a floppy only during read and write operations, when the drive is actually spinning. When no data transfers are taking place, the drive generally stops spinning until it's called on again for service.

What Can Go Wrong

As you can imagine, reading and writing data on a floppy disk requires precise alignment and timing. Data on track 10, sector 8 can be found only if the head can be moved precisely from one track to another. The location of a particular sector depends on the disk drive's timing and the information written on the disk.

Actually, finding data on a disk is not such a stab in the dark as this may seem. When a disk is formatted or initialized, track and sector markers are placed on the disk. The stepper motor must get the head close to the right spot, but the computer's operating system software can instruct the head to do a bit of searching if it's off the mark.

Dirty Heads. The most common problem you'll experience with a disk drive comes from the buildup of crud on a drive's read/write heads. Some of this is inevitable—it comes from the surface of your disks. The in-out motion of the read/write heads against the rotating disk results in removing tiny bits of the disk's

---

Behind Closed Doors

If you have single-sided disk drives, keep the disk drive door closed when they're not in use to guard against dust, which can destroy the read/write head. But don't do this if you have double-sided drives. If you shut the door without a disk inserted, the two read/write heads will press together, possibly damaging them. Instead, place a disk you no longer need into the drive, leaving it there with the door shut when the drive is not in use. This will protect the read/write heads from dust and from each other.

---

surface. No matter how clean you keep things, the heads pick up loose particles of the disk's coating. Generally, cheaper disks tend to be more of a problem. For that reason, you may want to use cheap disks as backups and for other purposes in which they won't be used frequently. Save more expensive disks for files you use day to day.

If you store your disks in the open (as opposed to keeping them in a box or closed file), they will pick up ambient contaminants. Dust, grime, and cigarette smoke that accumulate on disks are transferred to the heads during read/write operations. They may remain on the heads or may be transferred to another disk.

Dirty heads cause two problems. First, dirt directly interferes with the transfer of information to and from the heads. The grime simply gets in the way of the heads' operation. The second problem is that dirt can cause damage to both disks and heads. If there's dirt on a disk drive head, it can scratch a disk, wiping out whatever data were stored there. It also may cause the head itself to become scratched, making it difficult for the head to properly do its thing.

Timing and Alignment Problems. Because a disk drive depends on the accuracy of two motors (and often a belt, which connects the drive motor to the spindle shaft), timing and alignment problems are inevitable. But saying they're inevitable doesn't mean they are necessarily frequent. A disk drive that is kept clean and isn't abused can go for years of around-the-clock use without requiring timing or alignment adjustments.

In most cases, timing is a greater problem than alignment simply because the drive motor gets more wear and tear than the head-stepper motor. Drives that tie the motor to the spindle with a belt also have more problems because the belt eventually wears.

Bad Connections. As with other connections in your computer system, it is possible for a loose connection between the floppy disk controller and the drive to result in problems. The same is true for a weak or damaged line. While external disk drives would appear to be more susceptible to these kinds of problems, such problems are just as likely to occur with internal disk drives. The reason is that with internal drives, manufacturers often are forced to twist and bend ribbon cables into a variety of contorted shapes to route them from the disk controller to the drive. There isn't room to do otherwise. Over time these cables manage to work themselves free of the connectors to which they are supposed to be attached, or they simply break at a point where they have been severely strained.

A related problem with both internal and external drives is that the connecting cables can come into contact with other components where they may be subject to damage from heat or electrical interference.

Finally, dust and grime can get in the way of a proper connection. While a cable appears to be in contact with a circuit board connector, the connection may be blocked by the buildup of dirt.

Damaged Circuits. Disk drive circuits are as likely to be damaged as any other in your system. They can be short-circuited by loose solder, dirt, scratches, and just about anything else. They can be damaged by the buildup of heat. And they can be zapped by power surges or fouled up by individual component failure.

Heat. As we've said previously, heat causes electronic circuitry to behave in strange ways. This is as true for the circuits in your disk drive as it is for any other circuit. A special heat-related problem with disk drives is that heat expansion (or contraction due to cold) can throw off the precise alignments required to read and write data to and from a disk. The problem generally isn't that the drive components expand or contract but that the disk itself does. What used to be track 3 at 75 degrees Fahrenheit may become track 3½ when the temperature inside the computer approaches triple-digit levels. You still may be able to write onto the disk at the higher temperature, but you may not be able to locate data written at a cooler temperature.

Signs of Trouble

Drive-related problems rarely tend to be subtle. Pinning the problem down is not always easy, but it's generally not too difficult to determine whether a problem is drive-related or is rooted elsewhere in your computer system.

Here are some things that indicate possible disk drive problems.

Bad Connections. Most computers have built into the operating system a message that indicates whether a drive is connected or not. If you try reading from or writing to a disk drive and are informed the drive doesn't exist when you know it does, chances are there is a problem with the connection of that drive to the computer.

Reading Errors. If a drive has trouble reading from a disk, it's probably safest to assume the problem is with the disk before trying to chase down a disk drive problem. Some computer systems provide an error message that distinguishes between a bad disk and a disk drive failure. It will indicate you have a "bad sector," "bad disk," or something similar, or it will indicate something specific about a problem with the disk drive. When the software encounters an error reading, it instructs the disk drive to look around a bit in the vicinity of where the data are supposed to be located. If it still can't find the data, or if the data come across garbled, it will run a final test to see whether it can read some other data. If this is successful, the system knows the problem was caused by something peculiar to that file or to the specific sector of the file it was trying to read, rather than by the disk or the drive.

Not all systems have this level of sophistication built in. If your computer lacks such wizardry, you can run the same kind of test yourself by calling up a disk's directory and trying to read another file or by putting another disk into the drive. This kind of crude test should tell you whether the problem is with the file you are dealing with, the whole disk, or the drive (and possibly its connections to the floppy disk controller or the controller itself).

Writing Errors. If you appear to be able to write data onto a drive but have problems reading the data from the disk, chances are one of two things is happening: Either you stored the data you are now trying to read when the disk had expanded or contracted due to heat or cold, or expansion or contraction is taking place now, after you have stored the data. Because the disk has changed size, information that should be located in one place is somewhere else, and that somewhere else is outside the limits of error your computer permits.

Physical damage to the disk is another possibility. If you have trouble writing onto only a part of a disk, damage is the likely explanation. Some systems don't let you write anywhere on a disk after it detects what it believes to be damage. The system software flags the disk as "bad," and you must start again with a new—or at least different—floppy disk.

Pinning a problem down when you experience difficulty storing data on a disk involves essentially the same process you go through when you experience reading problems. If it is happening to only one disk and not to another, chances are the problem is with the disk and not with the disk drive. If it's happening to all disks, you've probably got a disk drive malfunction.

Timing and Alignment Errors. Timing errors tend to creep up on you. On one day you format a disk and store something on it. Meanwhile your disk drive's timing begins to get out of whack. A month or two down the line, you are unable to read something you've stored. For all practical purposes, the problem appears to be specific to the disk. But not necessarily. Another basic clue to a timing problem is whether errors seem to be tied only to disks formatted and written to sometime ago. It may be that you can store and read data on a newer disk because the disk drive is reading data at the same alignment (even if it's technically a *mis*alignment) at which they were originally stored. But older data can't be located because the alignment has changed significantly since they were last stored. If you can format a new disk and can read and write data from it, but you can't make any progress with more than one older disk, the problem is likely to be tied to timing or alignment.

Diagnostic Aids. There are a number of software packages available commercially and from public-domain software resources that can help you pin down disk- and drive-related problems. Some packages are designed to help you recover files from a damaged disk. Others guide you through the process of adjusting the timing and alignment of a drive. With the IBM PC and many IBM compatibles, software built into the operating system helps you recover files that have been lost through physical damage to the disk or through errors in the disk's formatting or directory information. There are programs similar to the MS-DOS/PC-DOS "RECOVER" command available for other systems, although these generally aren't built into operating systems.

Preventing Problems

There isn't much you can do to prevent timing and alignment problems. They are the natural consequences of machine wear and tear. The more you use the drive, the sooner you're likely to experience problems. Some newer computer systems can monitor disk drive wear and automatically compensate for it. Most other disk drive problems can be prevented through good housekeeping practices.

The most likely cause of a disk-related problem is a dirty read/write head. It will pick up dirt even from the air circulating through your computer, although most contaminants come in via disks—either little bits of the disk's coating or miscellaneous stuff that has accumulated on the disk because it was not stored or handled properly. Experience dictates that lower-priced disks tend to shed their coatings more easily than higher-priced disks. This doesn't mean, however, that you shouldn't buy cheap disks, just that they shouldn't be used for day-in, day-out work. Use them to store backup copies of programs and data files, and keep them in their boxes or in a covered file when not in use.

Disks shouldn't be stored where they will get excessively hot (more than 110 degrees Fahrenheit) or cold (below 50 degrees). On a hot summer day, the temperature in a car can get well above 125 degrees. You probably won't be able to read data on a disk

Don't Shake Your Head

When you move your computer from one place to another, there's a chance the drive's read/write head can become damaged from bouncing up and down. To avoid such problems, use a "head protection spacer" whenever you move. You can make one easily by cutting a piece of thin cardboard into the shape of a floppy disk. Or use a disk you no longer need.

that has experienced such heat, even after it cools down. If the disk gets sufficiently hot, it will become so distorted that it will never return to its original shape. Similar problems can arise when a disk gets too cold, although this isn't as likely. A good rule of thumb is to avoid storing disks at any temperature at which you would be uncomfortable yourself for long periods of time.

Any physical damage to a disk—such as scratching or otherwise marring the surface—can cause problems by literally gouging the data right off the disk's surface. This can happen if you write on a disk label with a ballpoint pen instead of with a felt marker or if you merely leave a disk lying about your desk, where things inevitably get piled on top of it.

Touching the disk surface with your fingers also damages the disk. First, you may directly transfer grease and grime from your hands. Second, that grease is sufficiently acidic to etch away the disk's surface. It's a good rule to keep your hands off the disk surface entirely, but there are times when you must align the center hole if you are having trouble getting it to work. There are no data stored here, so you are reasonably safe touching this area. Data are stored in the area exposed through the 1½"-long elliptical hole in the disk's jacket.

Data on a floppy are written magnetically. This means you can't expose your disks to any magnetic field without running the risk of losing stored data. You'd be surprised how many magnetic fields exist in your computer system, let alone outside it. Any electric motor works through magnetism, including those in your printer. There are magnetic fields surrounding transformers, including the one in your computer's power supply. There are magnets inside speakers, including the one inside your computer. A rather large magnetic field exists in a video monitor to guide information to the screen. Modems can generate sufficiently large magnetic fields to wipe out data on a disk, as can telephones when they ring. Don't overlook that electric pencil sharpener and your high-intensity desk lamp. Even fluorescent lights emit magnetic fields, but you needn't worry about this if disks are kept more than 6" away.

In short, disks belong in their jacket covers or inside a box or file, and the file itself ought to be on a shelf or table away from your computer system and any other electrical gadget.

More Reasons for Not Smoking. Everyone except the Tobacco Institute admits to the hazards of smoking. Those burning leaves not only coat your lungs with all kinds of strange stuff, they also dump it all over your disks and inside your disk drives. If you smoke, you can get a quick idea of what you are doing to your system by wiping your hand across the screen of your CRT. The same film you find there also coats disks and a disk drive's innards. The film can collect and retain dust and moisture, resulting in corrosion. Moreover, the film makes read/write head movement sluggish and increases the force required by the stepper motor, which could speed up wear on the disk drive. Your choices are to kick this nasty habit or to indulge yourself where you aren't constantly blowing smoke all over your disks and computer.

What You Can and Can't Do

You should be able to take care of most problems you'll experience with your disk drives, the most frequent one being a dirty read/write head. You won't be able to perform the drive alignment and make certain other adjustments without an oscilloscope, but some repairs require little more than a screwdriver and a little care.

Cleaning the Heads. There are a number of commercially available cleaning products designed to clean a disk drive's read/write heads. There is also a raging debate about whether these products do more harm than good. The standard commercial head-cleaning kit consists of what appears to be a normal floppy disk, except that instead of a coated Mylar surface there is a feltlike pad. You pour some magic potion onto this pad, place the disk into the disk drive, and activate the drive. The head presses down on the cleaning disk and is bathed as it passes over the moistened material. No after-bath talcum powder treatment is needed.

The debate about these cleaning kits is whether the process is too hard on the read/write head. If there is dirt on the head and it gets picked up by the cleaning pad, does the dirt scratch the head with each subsequent pass? Another concern is that the cleaning kits deposit moist goop on the read/write head, which is then deposited on the first disk you insert after cleaning.

There probably is no answer to this debate. The cleaning kits, while somewhat expensive, do offer convenience. You squirt a little fluid on the pad, plop it in the drive, activate the drive, and *presto*—a nice, clean head. The alternate approach requires that you remove the drive from its cabinet so you can clean the drive head directly. If your warranty doesn't prohibit cleaning kits (some do), if you follow a few precautions, and if you're willing to part with approximately $35, such kits are for you.

If you prefer cleaning kits, the lesson is to not use them to the point they become dirty themselves and can scratch the head. You also should use a clean, discarded disk in the drive after cleaning to minimize the possibility of depositing dirt on a perfectly good disk.

Cleaning Without a Kit. Take a look at a floppy disk. As you can see, the part where the head comes in contact with the disk is on the part of the disk farthest from where you put it into the disk drive. That means the read/write heads are on the far side of the drive and generally can't be reached from the front of the computer. So, if you want to clean the heads without a kit, you'll have to remove the drive from its cabinet. This is usually a pretty straightforward procedure.

On systems in which disk drives aren't built into the computer itself (such as the Apple II), all you have to do is unscrew the few screws that hold the drive in the cabinet. On other systems (such as the IBM PC), you must unfasten the central processing unit cabinet to get at the drives.

Once the drive is exposed, your goal is to remove as few things as possible to get to the heads. How far you must go depends on the drive's design. On some systems you can get directly at the heads from one side or the other. This is a bit difficult on machines such as the IBM PC, but don't despair—the worst you'll have to do is loosen the circuit board on top of the drive and maybe remove a cable or two.

As with any other disassembly operation, you are urged to make a sketch illustrating all that you plan to remove. Label cables with masking tape so you'll know where they're supposed to go.

The circuit board is likely held in place with four screws. To gain access to the heads, you'll probably have to remove one or more connectors so you can move the board out of the way. Decide in advance which ones you want to remove, and mark them directly (or at least indicate where they belong in your sketch). Be sure you know which way is "up"; in many cases you can install connectors either way, but only one way is correct. Simply stick a piece of masking tape on the connector as a flag indicating the "up" side.

OK, you're ready to go. Ground yourself to your machine (see Zapping Delicate Circuits, page 51), and carefully remove the appropriate screws and cables so you can get to the heads.

Once the heads are exposed, it's cleaning time. Your cleaning tools are a couple of cotton swabs and a bottle of isopropyl (rubbing) alcohol—about $1.50's worth of goods, available at any drugstore. If you have a single-sided disk drive, the head will be located under an arm that contains a head pad. With a double-sided drive, each head is on an arm. The head appears as a little piece of (white?) ceramic with one or two dark lines across it. To clean it, you'll probably need to move the arm out of the way. *Be very gentle:* It lifts up easily, but only so far. It's spring-loaded; if you let go, it will come flying back.

Dip a cotton swab in the alcohol, and press it against the inside of the bottle to wring out excess fluid. Gently wipe the head with the swab, being careful not to leave any cotton or other foreign matter on the head.

Take Care of Floppies

You will run into all kinds of warnings about how sensitive your floppy disks are to damage. The more you take these warnings to heart, the better. Here's a summary of floppy disk no-nos.

* Never touch the disk surface through the access hole—the elliptically shaped opening in the disk's cover where the actual reading and writing are done.
* Don't expose the disks to excessive heat or cold or to a magnetic field. Motors, telephones, and all sorts of other electrical devices—including your computer's power supply—generate magnetic fields.
* Don't write on your disks, paper-clip them, or otherwise gouge them. If you do, you'll physically damage the disk and, along with it, whatever programs or data were located there.
* Don't leave disks lying around—you are inviting trouble. They'll get dirty, crushed, or knocked onto the floor. They belong in their jackets, stored upright in a container that will keep dust from getting to them.
* Always maintain backup copies of programs and data. No matter how careful you are, something always seems to go wrong with a floppy—usually the one you forgot to back up.

Head Pads. On a single-sided disk drive, the head pad is used to push the disk against the head. (On a double-sided drive, the second head does this.) While you have the drive open, you should inspect the head pad. Even a relatively new pad will appear a little brownish, but if it's really dirty, it'll be obvious. A pad tends to wear on one side. It starts out white and is about 1/8″ to 1/4″ high. If it is filthy or worn, you should replace it, although that is easier said than done. There's no difficulty in removing the old pad and replacing it with a new one. The problem is finding a new pad.

DISK DRIVE
PRESSURE PAD

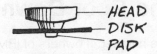

HEAD
DISK
PAD

Chances are that even if you live in a large town with a few well-stocked electrical supply stores that specialize in computer parts, you will have a hard time locating head pads. Your best bet is to call around, but be prepared to go directly to the manufacturer or its wholesale distributors. Some manufacturers are a bit nasty about having to deal with piddling little orders for a handful of $2.00 head pads. They like to take orders from trusted wholesalers and computer manufacturers that buy them by the gross. If they give you a hard time, insist that they put you in touch with a retailer who will help you. Once you find a source of pads, you should probably buy a dozen or so, just to avoid the hassle of finding them again someday.

By the way, you aren't likely to have any luck getting head pads from a computer store. If the store does repairs, it is almost sure to have some on hand, but the store's owners would rather have you part with $50 to $150 (or whatever they charge for disk drive cleaning) than to sell you a measly $2.00 pad. But if you have a good relationship with a dealer, this may be a good source.

Once you find the head pads, study them. Opposite each pad are two plastic prongs. You must squeeze these together to get the old pad out of its holder in the head pad arm; then squeeze the prongs again to install the new pad. The only way to do this is with small needle-nose pliers. Avoid touching the pad with your fingers (your body oils will rub off on the pad, damaging disks you later insert) and yanking the arm around (it will break off at the slightest provocation). You shouldn't have to force anything, so go gently.

There's one more thing you should do, as long as you have taken the drive apart: Clean the disk drive assembly. Using a trusty vacuum cleaner, suck out all the dust and dirt. Check all cable connections to make sure everything fits properly. You may

If You Break
the Door Down

A disturbingly large number of owners of IBM personal computers using Tandon disk drives have had the misfortune of having a disk drive door break or simply fall off. Worse yet, no replacement parts are available from Tandon or IBM. One solution, however, is to use the door from an Apple disk drive; Apple does make the parts available. The door looks almost identical to the Tandon door and fits almost precisely; to fit perfectly, it needs a thin shim between the door hinge and the cone lever arm to which it is mounted.

wish at this time to check the timing (see page 88). If not, replace the circuit board and cables and put the drive back in its cabinet, but *don't yet put a good disk in the drive.*

Before you certify the job as well done, turn your machine on to see how things sound. Using a disk you no longer need, request a directory listing for the drives you just cleaned and see if everything appears to work well. Now take a disk without any data on it and format or initialize it. This gives you a chance to be certain that everything is OK without exposing your data to any problems resulting from your putting things back together improperly. If everything checks out, continue to proceed with caution by making your first action a read rather than a write operation. If everything's OK, you're back in business.

How Often to Clean. How often you clean your disk drive heads depends on how much you use your computer and to what sorts of environmental garbage you expose it. Generally, you probably will get about five hundred hours' use out of a disk drive before you must clean the heads. This assumes pretty heavy use —a lot of reading and writing. If you spend five hundred hours sitting in front of your machine composing your memoirs, with a keystroke here and a keystroke there, chances are you'll get two to three times this use before it's cleaning time. The real key to when to clean the heads is when you have problems. If it ain't broken, don't fix it!

Cleaning Cassette Tape Drives. While cassette recorders are rapidly disappearing as storage media for personal computers, some are still in use.

Given the under-$50 cost of most such machines, repairs are likely to be minimal; if it breaks, you're better-off getting a new one. About the only thing you'll ever need or want to do is to clean the unit's read/write heads. Almost any problem beyond this will cost you more than $50 to track down and fix.

If you experience problems reading and writing to and from a cassette and all your cables are properly attached, chances are the problem is either the tape or a dirty read/write head. Try replacing the tape—in fact, stick your favorite music cassette in the unit —and see whether this works. If it does, but the sound is distorted, clean the play/record heads with a cotton swab using isopropyl (rubbing) alcohol. If the tape's speed sounds off, you should also "de-glaze" all the rubber capstans (small, black, donut-shaped wheels) that come in contact with the tape. Simply wipe them off with an alcohol-dipped swab.

Cleaning Disks. You shouldn't have to clean the disks themselves if they are properly stored and you don't touch the exposed areas. But the inevitable may someday occur: Junior (or the dog or your neighbor Fred) comes along with raspberry jam all over his fingers (or paws) and picks up the disk that contains your life's literary masterpiece.

You can't stick it in your machine like that, but you aren't willing to pitch the disk and start back at Chapter One. Generally, you don't *want* to recover a disk like this, but if you didn't bother to make a backup copy of the disk, you'll have no other choice. Take your cotton swab and alcohol, and clean the disk surface. Be very careful not to scratch the disk in the process and even more careful not to push the jam under the disk's jacket.

Don't overdo the alcohol, but don't use too little, either. How much is enough? You want to get the disk wet enough to ensure you don't have to scrape it to remove the foreign substance but not so wet that you end up floating the substance under the jacket. If you get any of this mess under the jacket, resign yourself to losing the disk. It is likely that anything trapped under the jacket will scratch the disk surface, wiping out your data—and probably messing up the drive head.

Cleaning a disk should be a last resort—one you hope you never encounter.

Timing. Even if you keep your disks and drives clean, use good disks, and don't cheat the IRS, you'll still need to adjust the timing of your disk drive someday. Adjusting the timing is about a fifteen-minute operation, not much harder than cleaning the disk drive heads. Anytime you do one job you probably should do the other, because the major effort is getting to the drive, not doing the cleaning or the timing.

A few manufacturers of larger computers have been very nice —they have cut a little hole in the cabinetry under the disk drive that is covered by a small plate that plops out to expose the timing disk. This makes it a fairly simple job to adjust the timing.

Unfortunately, no personal computers have these convenient little cutouts, so you have two choices: get a diagnostic disk that displays timing errors and adjustments on your screen, or pull the drive out of its cabinet so you can see the timing disk.

There are disk-diagnostic software packages available—many in the public domain—that allow you to simply insert a disk and analyze many aspects of a drive's performance, including timing. All you do is follow instructions.

DISK DRIVE TIMING WHEEL

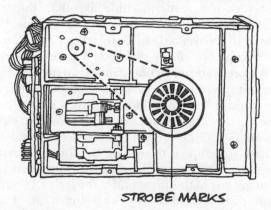

STROBE MARKS

You can adjust the timing without a diagnostic disk, however. To do this, you must expose the timing disk and locate the adjusting potentiometer, or "pot," a variable resistor much like the volume control on your TV. The timing disk is very obvious. It is located on the side of the drive opposite the control circuit board. The disk is round and marked off with alternate bands of black and white. Usually there are two bands: one for 60-cycle current, which is used in the United States, the other for the 50-cycle current found overseas.

LOCATION OF TIMING POT

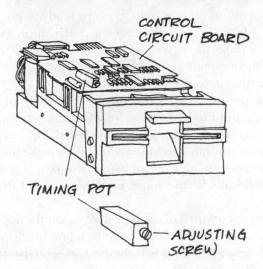

CONTROL
CIRCUIT BOARD

TIMING POT

ADJUSTING
SCREW

Locating the correct pot is a bit more difficult because there are generally at least two of them on a drive. Typically, the pot you want will be on the circuit board on top of the drive, but some manufacturers tuck it away elsewhere.

The only way you can determine which is the correct pot without a manufacturer's manual is by experimenting. This puts a real premium on making a diagram of exactly what you are doing and keeping it, so you don't have to experiment the next time the timing needs adjusting.

As usual, mark down with paper and pencil what you are pulling apart, and appropriately label any cables you disconnect. You are looking for a couple of mounting screws that hold your drive in place. Once you can move the drive, you must get it positioned so that you can: see the timing disk, adjust the pot, and not short the whole thing out.

To adjust the timing, you must have your system turned on. Be careful—chances are you are dealing with relatively low-voltage direct current, but you may be poking around areas with a lot more juice. Moreover, even relatively low-voltage DC can zap a circuit or a delicate integrated circuit, so be very careful not to short things out.

Once you've found a pot or two, you are ready to go. You can get a plastic adjusting tool for under a dollar at an electronic supply shop. It looks like a screwdriver but has the advantage of not being made of metal, which can cause a short circuit. A small screwdriver is fine if you're careful.

The first step is to mark down on paper which pot you are going to adjust and how it is set. The adjusting screw probably has a blob of stuff that looks a lot like hardened fingernail polish. You may or may not have to knock this off to make any adjustments. Its purpose is to lock the adjustment once it is made at the factory, but it usually breaks loose easily when you turn the adjusting screw.

If you are working with a diagnostic disk, select the appropriate timing test. You'll see either a message or a graphic display indicating how close your timing is to being correct. Give the pot a half turn one way or the other and see what happens. If nothing happens, you likely have the wrong pot. If so, turn the pot back to its original position and try the other. When you see a response, does your turning bring the drive closer to or further from the correct timing? Eventually you'll know which is the correct pot and which way you must turn it to get the timing right. Write that information down in your maintenance log (see page 31).

If you don't have a diagnostic disk, you can still do the timing adjustment, but you'll need a 60-cycle timing light. Don't despair, they are quite inexpensive. In fact, ordinary fluorescent light bulbs are 60-cycle timing lights—they go on and off 60 times a second. The only problem you may face with this approach is getting the drive positioned so its circuits aren't touching metal and placing yourself so you can see the timing disk and still get to the pot. Turn off the computer's power before you start.

Once everything is in place and the power is turned back on, activate the drive. If you are a programmer, you can put together a little routine to constantly read a file, but you needn't go that far. Just sticking a disk in and requesting its directory or index will get things moving enough to enable you to make the necessary adjustments.

The timing is off if the timing marks appear to be moving. Your goal is to adjust the pot until the marks appear to be standing still.

The final step in adjusting the timing is to take a little fingernail polish and dab it on the pot adjusting screw—and nowhere else. This keeps the pot from vibrating out of adjustment. The trick is to let the polish dry a bit before putting it on the adjusting screw. If it's too wet, you're likely to end up with fingernail polish in places it shouldn't be. If you let it get too dry, you won't be able to dab it on at all. You may want to experiment first on a piece of paper. (If you want to go the whole nine yards, there are a number of "liquid lock" products available at a local electronics store, but fingernail polish works just fine.)

Once again, don't expose your precious data or programs to possible damage. Test your timed drive with a blank disk. Start by formatting or initializing it, write something to it, and then read it back to see if everything is working.

Alignment. If cleaning the heads, adjusting the timing, and checking out the disk drive's wires and connections leaves you with a problem, chances are the drive's alignment is off.

Adjusting the alignment is no more difficult than setting the timing, but you need an oscilloscope to do it. A suitable oscilloscope probably costs more than a disk drive, so if alignment turns out to be the problem, you can either ship your disk drive off to the manufacturer or to a repair shop for adjustment or even buy a new disk drive. Either way, you'll spend less than the price of an oscilloscope.

Check around locally. Many computer repair services offer fairly good prices on disk drive repairs. If you can't find one that

Hard Facts
About Hard Disks

The speed at which disk capacity has grown is one of the many wonders of microcomputer technology. It has been only a few years since an 8″ floppy disk could hold only 100,000 characters. Now some are capable of storing ten times that amount. At that same time, minicomputer systems had enormous cabinets housing 20-megabyte hard disk drives that were far more delicate than newborn babies.

The cabinet space that once held a couple hundred kilobytes of floppy disk storage now routinely holds 10 to 20 megabytes. With the speed at which the technology is changing it wouldn't be unrealistic to expect these capacities to double in the not-too-distant future.

What made these developments possible is the Winchester hard disk drive. The first hard disks were so delicate that a little too much dust, smoke, or other airborne particles was enough to bring a disk to a crashing halt. These weren't soft landings either. When a disk crashed, it crashed.

Some engineers at IBM got the idea of sealing the part of the drive that contained the disk platters and read/write heads. This virtually eliminated the problems of head crashes due to environmental contamination.

Hard Disk Problems

The main problems with Winchester disk drives result from banging them around and from electrical surges. But despite their delicate nature relative to floppies, Winchesters are

does, some computer stores offer the service, or you may be able to find a reliable and reasonably priced free-lance technician through a local computer users' group. If you can't find someone locally, check out computer magazines. There are a number of organizations specializing in disk drive service for around $35 to more reliable than floppies simply because the media are not exposed to the same environmental hazards.

External hard disk problems, such as defective control circuitry and bad cabling, are similar to those found with floppies and can be fixed in the same way. Because of their design, however, there is no way for you or your local computer technician to get inside a Winchester to repair it. Winchesters are assembled in "clean rooms"—and we mean clean. It's certainly possible to open a Winchester, but without being able to maintain a near-sterile environment such action would almost certainly result in its contamination and subsequent crash.

Preventing Problems

While you are very limited in what you can do if you have a problem, you can do a lot to prevent it in the first place. You should burn a hard disk drive in while it's still under warranty, for example. As hard as they try not to, manufacturers let a few defective disks slip through. Unless you want to shell out money for a replacement, you should run your drive through an intensive burn-in right away.

While it's true that you are likely to experience fewer problems with a hard disk than with a floppy, you stand to lose a lot more if the thing breaks. This puts a premium on religiously backing up your hard disk files on tape or floppies. Doing this once a week isn't too often. Important files or programs should be backed up immediately.

Although the media and read/write heads are sealed, cleanliness is still important. Keep dust and grime away from your hard disk control circuitry and power, data, and control cables and connections.

$75 a drive, depending on the type you have. It's possible your local computer store ships its drives to one of these outfits. By sending your drive directly, you may save the few bucks in markup the store charges you for doing this.

6
INTERFACES

Your computer, as we've said, is a pretty reliable beast. With care, and a bit of luck, you may never have to deal with most problems covered in this book. Care and luck, however, only go so far when it comes to computer interfaces.

There's probably nothing more frustrating than trying to hook up a printer, modem, or other computer peripheral and not having it work properly. Two devices advertised to be "compatible" simply aren't when it comes time to plug them in and go to work. The simple fact is that among the biggest lies in the world of personal computing are "it's IBM compatible," "it's RS-232 compatible," and some similar claims. Don't believe them.

There are no easy answers as to why computer peripherals don't work right when you hook them together. But a little understanding of how things are *supposed* to work can go a long way toward avoiding frayed nerves—and costly trips to a repair shop.

Bits and Bytes

The first thing to understand is how data travel from one device to another.

Information—programs and data—is stored in your computer as strings of "1s" and "0s," representing plus and minus voltage levels, high and low voltages, "set" and "reset" conditions, or other binary choices on which computers operate. Each binary condition represents a single bit, with groups of eight bits representing one byte. (The precise details aren't too important—it's the concept that counts, so don't lose any sleep over this.)

Data typically are stored in an eight-bit byte. The letter *a*, for example, is represented in your computer in the sequence 01001001. This is by convention; the letter *a* could just as well be any combination of "1s" and "0s" that people agree upon as representing *a*. The most common convention governing how we represent numbers, letters, punctuation marks, special symbols, and other characters used in communications or document formatting is known as ASCII, for American Standard Code for Information Interchange.

OK, you ask, we said that data are stored as eight bits, but the ASCII code for *a* really has only seven bits. This isn't a contradiction. The eighth bit is reserved for a rudimentary error-checking technique known as "parity." (Your word processing program also may make use of the eighth bit to indicate extra spaces or "soft" line returns.)

The parity bit is added at the front of the sequence of "1s" and "0s." It, too, is either a "1" or a "0," depending on whether the parity is "even" or "odd." When you transmit data using "even parity," for example, the computer counts the number of "1s" in the ASCII code of each character. (For example, the ASCII code for *a*—1001001—has three "1s.") If the total is not an even number, an additional "1"—the parity bit—is added to produce an even number of "1s." If the ASCII code already has an even number of "1s," a "0" is added as the parity bit. "Odd parity" works the opposite way: Each character must have an odd number of "1s." You can also use no parity, in which the parity bit is simply ignored.

So much for parity. There's also the notion of "parallel" versus "serial" communications. If you want to transmit the letter *a* from a computer to a printer, there are two choices. You can march the seven data bits and a parity bit down a single line, one after the other, to your printer (serial communications), or you can send all eight bits simultaneously down eight separate wires (parallel communications). Think of it as the difference between eight cars driving down a one-lane highway compared with an eight-lane highway.

Parity is just for starters. You also need a way to determine whether the printer is ready to receive your data, along with some agreed-upon arrangement for marking where a character begins

PARALLEL VS. SERIAL COMMUNICATION

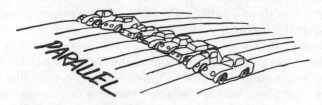

SERIAL

EIGHT BITS TRANSMITTED ONE AT A TIME

EIGHT BITS TRANSMITTED SIMULTANEOUSLY

and ends. For reasons not important here, you may wish to have the communications occur in both directions simultaneously or in just one direction at a time. A printer and computer also must agree on whether the first bit sent will be the right-most bit in the byte or the left-most.

So far we've got a pretty complicated scheme. But wait, there's more. It's not enough to have the right wires connected properly; you also need the software at both ends working together. If a computer transmits seven data bits and calls it an *a,* a printer must receive the same seven bits and recognize it as an *a.* If a computer is set up to transmit seven data bits and an eighth parity bit but a printer is looking for eight data bits, the transmitted *a* will be received as a special character or symbol, not the letter intended.

As you can see, transmitting data between two computer devices represents a hornet's nest of potential problems. Let's look at a few.

RS-232 and Other Lies

If you've read computer product specifications or advertisements, you've probably heard the term "RS-232." RS-232 is a very loose standard promulgated by the Electronic Industries Association. The standard defines a 25-line cable and a few rules about the voltage levels that will indicate a binary "1" or "0." Most computers have a standard RS-232 serial port. Most modems do, too. Your printer may or may not be RS-232 compatible.

What is RS-232 all about? It's all about a lot of problems.

The biggest problem with the RS-232 standard is that computer equipment manufacturers are pretty free to set it up any way they want. There are rules about which piece of equipment must be the "data terminal equipment" (DTE), in the jargon of computers, and which piece of equipment is the "data communications equipment" (DCE). In the world of RS-232, the computer is the DTE and the peripheral (printer, modem, whatever) is the DCE. These rules help determine which end gets to talk on which of the up to 25 lines going between a computer and a peripheral. The lines are referred to by the number of the pin at which they terminate.

DTEs, for example, are supposed to transmit on pin 2 (transmitted data) and receive on pin 3 (received data). Data communications equipment should have the opposite configuration.

It's not that simple, of course.

The problem is that RS-232 is such a loose standard that, in many cases, a regular 25-pin connector (also referred to as a "DB-25 connector") actually will have wires attached to only nine pins. Indeed, you can have a DB-25 connector, with 25 wires in the cable, with only one wire connected. All of this, mind you, is between components that are "RS-232 compatible." Under the RS-232 rules, virtually anything can be deemed "RS-232 compatible." That's no guarantee, however, that one RS-232–compatible device will communicate correctly with another.

It should be pretty clear at this point that good old RS-232 is nothing short of a mess. But there's still more. (See page 102.)

What Do
All Those Pins Do?

Understanding cables is difficult at best. It may help, however, to understand what happens (or is supposed to happen) on each of the principal lines of a standard RS-232 serial or Centronics parallel cable. With such an understanding, you may gain the insight necessary to sort out the problem you confront. One problem, however, is that the "official" definitions of what the various lines do is tied to the idea of one end of the cable being a computer and the other end being a modem.

RS-232 Pins

When an RS-232 cable is used to connect up something other than a modem, some of the definitions don't make much sense. A manufacturer may use an RS-232 cable to attach a serial printer to a computer, for example. The printer's designers want it to be able to tell the computer when the printer is out of paper, so a common line, such as line 8 ("Data Carrier Detect"), is selected for this. The result is that the "standard" definition of line 8 is mislabeled.

Below are the most commonly used lines. There are 25 lines in all. Most are rarely used, but a printer manufacturer may use any of these to provide information to the computer. If you have an RS-232 connection between something other than a computer and a modem, you must read the manufacturers' manuals to see how they intend some of these signals to be used.

Pin 1: Chassis Ground (CG). This is a safety line. Its purpose is to provide a ground for the cable to prevent damage to equipment at either end of the cable in the event of a short circuit. In spite of the obvious value of this line, it is often not used.

Pin 2: Transmit Data (TD). A computer "talks" on line 2 and "listens" on line 3. A modem does the opposite. Sometimes a printer or computer is configured to act like a modem. If so, both devices will try to talk on the same line and listen on a line on which no one is talking. A null modem cable, which reverses lines 2 and 3, solves the problem of both ends being configured the same way.

Pin 3: Receive Data (RD). This is where a computer should listen for incoming data and a modem should talk.

Pin 4: Request to Send (RTS). This is a signal from the computer to the modem, asking it to prepare itself to transmit data over the line.

Pin 5: Clear to Send (CTS). When the modem is ready to send data over the phone, it signals the computer on this line.

Pin 6: Data Set Ready (DSR). The modem lets the computer know it is ready to go by signaling over this line. This is a bit different than pin 5 ("Clear to Send"). CTS indicates that the modem has a phone link and is ready to retransmit data it receives from the computer. DSR simply lets the computer know the modem is ready to get rolling—it isn't off running self-tests or doing something else. But it doesn't necessarily mean the modem is ready to send anything over the line.

Pin 7: Signal Ground (SG). The voltage of a particular circuit is measured against a reference. This is necessary because with voltage it takes two to tango—you don't technically have a voltage reading without two points in a circuit. Pin 7 provides that second point, used as a reference against which all other pins' signals are measured. (Pin 1, "Chassis Ground," is a protective circuit only; it doesn't play an active role in the communications process.)

Pin 8: Data Carrier Detect (DCD). This signal from the modem lets the computer know the modem has received something that it recognizes as a valid modem signal. If you called another computer and a person, rather than a modem, answered, this signal would be off. The modem doesn't recognize the human voice as a valid modem signal.

Pin 20: Data Terminal Ready (DTR). This signal from the computer to the modem is similar to pin 6 ("Data Set Ready"). It is used to prepare the modem to be hooked into the phone system. It is generally not turned on until the DSR signal is on.

Pin 22: Ring Indicator (RI). When the modem hears the phone ringing, it turns this signal on to let the computer know there is an incoming call.

A final word about the names and abbreviations used above: You will find different versions. "Transmit Data" (TD), for example, also may be abbreviated as TDX, XD, DX, or anything else that strikes the fancy of a manufacturer's manual writer. Even more frustrating, you'll find manufacturers doing things like having their modems transmit data on line 8 or otherwise mix the standard RS-232 lines. There is no good reason for this.

Centronics Pins

The basic operation of a Centronics interface is similar to that of an RS-232, except that data are transferred in parallel rather than in serial. This means that eight bits are sent at once, side by side, rather than one bit at a time.

The Centronics standard was developed for printers, while RS-232 was set up for communications between a computer and a modem. As a result, Centronics control lines serve very different functions from those of RS-232.

Note that there are two lines for every function, a system of signal redundancy used by Centronics interfaces to provide for two-way communications.

Pin 1/19: Data Strobe. A strobe is sent on line 1 from the computer to the printer as a signal that an eight-bit byte of data has been placed on the eight data lines (see below).

Pin 19 is used by the printer to do the same thing when it needs to communicate back to the computer.

Pin 11/29: Busy. The signal on pin 11 is from the printer. It tells the computer that the printer is up and running. The computer uses pin 29 to communicate the same status message to the printer.

Pin 10/28: Acknowledge. After the printer has successfully captured a byte from the data lines, it acknowledges its readiness to accept another by signaling the computer on pin 10. The computer does the same to the printer on pin 28.

Pins 2 through 9 and Pins 20 through 27: Data Lines. The computer sends eight data bits at a crack to the printer on pins 2 through 9. It receives data from the printer on pins 20 through 27.

Pin 15/14: Forms Control (VFU-Vertical Formatting Unit). This line is used by the computer to control form-length selection for printers with a mechanical formatting unit.

Pin 12: Paper Error. Pin 12 lets the printer tell the computer when it is out of paper.

Pin 16/33: Signal Ground. This line is the same as the RS-232 pin 7—a reference line against which all the other signals are measured.

Pin 18: +5 Volts. A +5-volt power line.

Pin 17: Chassis Ground. Comparable to RS-232 pin 1. This is a safety line.

Pins 13, 32: Select. Signals through these pins from the printer to the computer let the latter know that the former is on-line. These pins can be used in conjunction with other pins, such as pin 12, to provide other status messages.

The remaining pins are rarely used.

While there is nothing in the RS-232 standard that specifies whether a plug or cable should be male or female, conventions have evolved in this regard. It is pretty standard to have the cable's connectors male with the receptacle's ports female. Pretty simple, right? Unfortunately, the RS-232 port on the back of an IBM PC asynchronous communications adapter is male. Does that mean the RS-232 cable you purchased with your printer won't work? Maybe, maybe not. It's anyone's guess; no one seems to follow the rules. It isn't a lost cause, however. Most electronics stores can supply you with the appropriate adapter or even make one up at little cost.

Getting the right signals on the right lines is no guarantee that two machines can communicate. Let's assume for a moment that you have the proper cable, lines, and pins and everything is in RS-232 heaven. Let's go further and assume your computer and its peripheral—say, your printer—are communicating over the correct lines. Is there any guarantee things will work properly?

Far from it.

For one thing, there must be agreements between the two devices on a number of issues. For example: At what rate will data be sent? How will the printer acknowledge receipt of data? Will the computer send seven- or eight-bit characters? What signals will the printer send to indicate it needs a break because it can't handle any more data? How will it tell the computer to begin sending after a break?

These sorts of issues must be resolved before things will work properly. Otherwise, you can have a completely proper physical setup and still not have a working interface.

Worse still, your word processing program's manual may tell you that the keyboard combination "ALT 146" will print the diphthong *ae*. That's great if your printer's software knows this, too. But the printer's software might tell the printer that "ALT 146" means "turn printer off." Clearly, this is no game for anyone with a weak stomach.

This confuses and frustrates even so-called experts, so don't be intimidated. By systematically evaluating what is going on, chances are you can solve a communications problem between two machines and do it just as fast as someone who has a degree in electronic engineering from an Ivy League school. The key is to be systematic.

Types of Serial Interfaces

There are several common RS-232 configurations. By examining them and comparing them with your own cable, you'll get a pretty good idea of how your equipment should be connected. In the discussion below, we'll assume the DTE is a computer and the DCE is a printer or modem. The computer also is referred to as a "terminal" and the printer or modem as a "data set." There's no magic in these terms, but you may find them in your documentation; in many cases, they are used incorrectly.

Three-Wire Interface. The minimum configuration possible for two-way RS-232 communications is a three-wire interface. As you can see from the figure on page 104, the three lines connect pins 2, 3, and 7. Pin 2 is the line on which the DTE transmits data to the DCE. Pin 3 is where the DCE *receives* information from the DTE. Pin 7 is necessary to provide a reference voltage for the other two lines.

This bare-bones RS-232 circuit may be used for communications. It would not allow any hardware handshaking—communications about such things as whether both machines are ready to receive data. But, if that's not a problem, you can communicate on this circuit with relative ease.

Null Modems. When is a modem not a modem? When it's a "null modem." How this beastie got its name isn't important. What's important to know is that a null modem is nothing more than a cable with lines 2 and 3 crisscrossed. This is necessary when both the computer and the modem or printer are configured by their respective manufacturers as DTEs or DCEs. By crossing lines, you avoid having both machines communicating on the same line. Frequently a null modem also has a number of "jumpers," which set up the appropriate substitutes for handshaking. For example, the "Request to Send" pin will be jumpered to the "Clear to Send" pin, a signal that should be coming from communications equipment. Similarly, "Data Terminal Ready" can be hooked to "Data Set Ready."

What all this jumpering accomplishes is that each machine feeds itself the signals it needs. Example: Many times a computer

ECONOMY RS·232

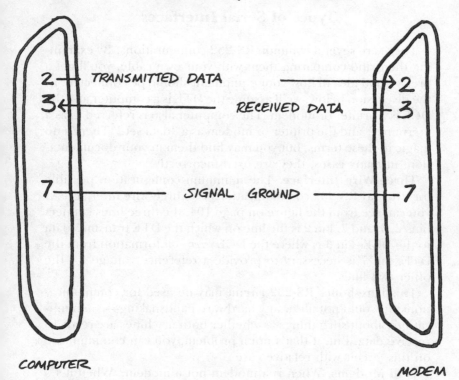

COMPUTER   MODEM

will transmit a signal on its "Request to Send" (RTS) line and wait until the modem sends a response on its "Clear to Send" (CTS) line before sending a character. If you hook the computer's RTS pin to its own CTS pin, it will always get a "Clear to Send" signal anytime it sends a "Request to Send."

While these minimal configurations work, they won't be very efficient. Probably the most common RS-232 circuit begins with full two-way communications—pin 2 for transmitting, pin 3 for receiving data. Next, pin 4 is included so the computer can signal when it is ready to send, and pin 5 is used so the printer or modem can let the computer know it is clear to send. Pins 6 and 20 provide general indicators of the readiness of both machines. Pin 20 indicates "Data Terminal Ready" and the peripheral's

NULL MODEM

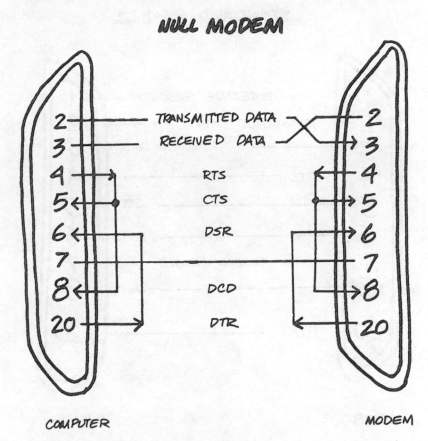

COMPUTER   MODEM

signaling "Data Set Ready" on pin 6. Pin 7 is used to provide a reference voltage against which all other signals are matched.

For a printer circuit, you could stop here, with pin 1 possibly included as "Protective Ground." If you connect a computer and a modem, you need two additional lines coming from the modem. These are pin 8, "Data Carrier Detect," to let the computer know the modem has established communications with another unit, and pin 22, "Ring Indicator," which enables the modem to tell the computer it has detected a telephone ring signal.

This full-blown RS-232 full-duplex (two-way communications) circuit provides all the signals necessary for communications and control over the flow of data between a DTE and a DCE. Because

STANDARD RS-232

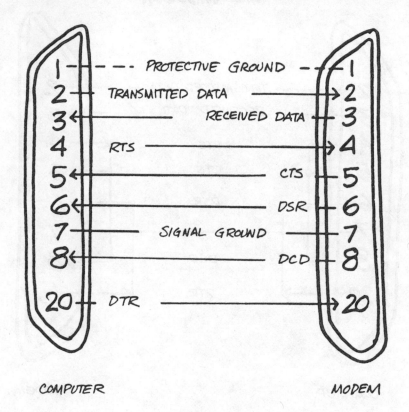

COMPUTER   MODEM

there are up to 25 lines in an RS-232 circuit, there are plenty left to allow for additional communications on other matters— whether the printer has paper, for example. Some of the unused lines have no specific purpose or are rarely used for the purpose for which they were originally intended. As a result, you can count on digging deeply into your documentation to find out what is going on with any of these additional lines.

You should see many opportunities here for troubleshooting. Let's assume that nothing at all is happening between your computer and printer. On the computer side, you could jump pin 4 to pin 5 ("Request to Send" to "Clear to Send"). This would constantly signal the computer that the printer is ready to receive data as soon as the computer asks whether it can send data. This is so because the computer's request is fed right back to its own pin 4 ("Request to Send"). Similarly, you could jump pin 6 to pin 20 on the printer side to tell your printer that the computer is working.

Parallel Interfaces

By now you probably are convinced that serial communications can be a real problem. You're right. Fortunately, parallel communications are a lot easier to deal with. The reason is that there are two common parallel interfaces and both are rather rigidly defined, at least compared to RS-232.

Most common is the Centronics interface, named after the printer manufacturer that developed it. The other, far more rigid, interface is known as IEEE-488. With the notable exception of Commodore and Osborne computers, there aren't many personal computer manufacturers using IEEE-488, primarily because it is relatively expensive to implement. A 6-foot IEEE-488 cable can set you back $75 or more, compared with $25 to $50 for a 25-foot RS-232 cable.

Simply put, parallel interfaces provide enough lines for a computer to transmit eight bits at once (in parallel), rather than sending them one after the other (serially). Parallel interfaces usually come in a 36-pin configuration; the 16 data lines enable bidirectional communications—eight bits in each direction. Like its serial counterparts, the parallel standards have several lines devoted to handshaking, the signals that permit the two machines to inform each other about various conditions.

There are three key signals sent during parallel communications: "Strobe," "Acknowledge," and "Busy." When a printer is not ready to receive data or is tied up printing previously transmitted data, it signals the computer with the "Busy" line. The computer lets the printer know when it has sent a character over the data lines by sending "Strobe." And the printer tells the computer it has received a character by transmitting "Acknowledge." There may be other lines, but they generally aren't vital. Most are used by the printer to report various error conditions.

CENTRONICS

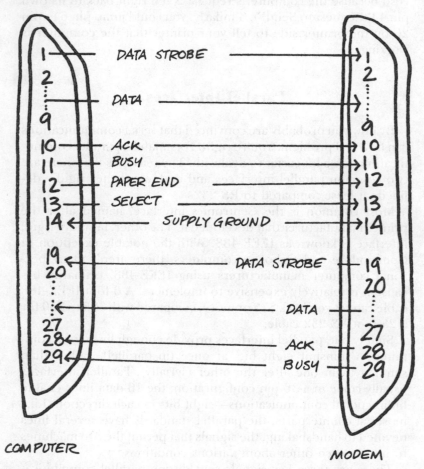

COMPUTER

MODEM

While things are a little more straightforward in the world of parallel communications, confusion can still reign. Most products on the market billed as "Centronics compatible" are just that. They are compatible, but that doesn't mean that they adhere completely to the standard. They use eight lines for data. "Strobe" is true when it is negative rather than positive. The same is true for the "Acknowledge" line. But this may not always be the case despite marketing slogans about "compatibility."

If there are problems, they most likely result from one machine being set up to support more control signals than the other. Your printer, for example, may fire off signals such as "Printer Error" and "Fault," but its cable may be missing these lines or the computer may not be set up to monitor them. While there are fewer hardware problems with parallel communications, you may encounter software incompatibilities. Both computer and printer must agree on how to interpret a character when it is transmitted, for example, and respond to various control signals consistently. (See What Do All Those Pins Do? on page 98.)

Troubleshooting

When two computer devices won't communicate, the first step is to wade through the devices' manuals to be absolutely certain you set up everything properly. This may sound like simplistic advice, but surprisingly few people bother with this when problems arise. Inevitably, you'll find that a printer has a series of switches that must be set to make it compatible with a computer. The same may be true of a modem or other peripheral. Be aware, however, that many devices permit you to make such changes in the computer's communications or operating software. Thus, while you may set your printer switches to receive data at 1,200 baud, your software may override this setting, sending data at 300 baud.

This Is a Test. Many printers and modems are set up to let you conduct tests that are independent of the computer. By doing this, you needn't have a device connected to the computer to run the printer or modem through its paces. If your printer or modem has this feature, you should make this your second step. It enables you to rule out the possibility of a faulty printer or modem before you begin tearing cables apart and cursing unreadable documentation.

How you proceed with either serial or parallel interface problems beyond this stage depends upon exactly what is going on. Is your printer printing nothing, or is it merely printing things wrong? If it's printing nothing, it probably means you really need

DIP SWITCHES

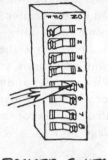
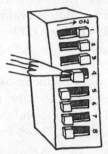

ROCKER SWITCH   SLIDE SWITCH

to look into things. If it's simply not working correctly, it is more likely a sign of incorrect switch settings or software problems.

A Friend, Indeed. Whether dealing with serial or parallel interfaces, the next most likely source of problems is with improper wiring or short circuits between two or more pins. If you've made your own cable, this may be the problem. But you can't rule out the possibility of wires gone astray even with a cable put together by pros.

You don't want to take apart your cable if you don't have to, so before proceeding, make sure you have all switches and software set properly. Without question, the best way to do this is to have a friend check things for you. Go through the settings step-by-step, explaining each time what you have done and why. Have your friend double-check. If you've goofed, it will be obvious. Don't be embarrassed, be happy.

Inspecting the Cable. If switches are properly set, you're certain the software is directing its output to the proper port, and things still aren't working right, it's time to check the cable for obvious flaws. You should disconnect the cable completely from the two devices before beginning this process to avoid any electrical hazard to yourself or your equipment. This also is the time to check the connection itself to be certain the cable is properly connected to each device. Look especially for a snug fit, and be sure there are no broken or bent pins on a male connector. If you can unscrew the connector cover, remove it and take a look inside. If the cover is sealed, you'll have to skip the next set of tests.

Under the cover, look for loose wires or sloppy soldering that may have inadvertently linked two or more pins. Tug on the lines gently to make sure the wires are attached properly. Male connectors generally have little lugs wrapped around the wires. Others are set up with female sockets into which the wires (usually with lugs over the wire ends) are inserted. They may be soldered in place. It won't hurt to pull them out if they aren't soldered as long as you put them back in the correct sockets.

If you have a clamp-on connector, don't open it; opening these can be tricky business, likely to result in something breaking. These connectors work by clamping the wires in the cable. Opening and reclosing the clamps may result in your ruining the cable or fouling up a connection, so hold on for a moment.

What Goes Where. Before you continue testing, sit down and make a drawing of which pin is connected to which wire. Take your time with this; a mistake can cost you hours of grief and an almost certain trip to a repair shop. You can use a copy of the chart below to copy everything. Starting at one end, write down the color of the cable and to which pin it is connected. This can get a little bit tricky for several reasons.

If you look carefully, you'll find the pin numbers stamped into the plastic on the front of the connector opposite the side where wires are attached. On the Centronics interface, pins are numbered from the lower left to the lower right, then from the upper left to the upper right. There is a total of 36 pins—1 through 18 on the bottom and 19 through 36 on the top. With a 25-pin RS-232 connector, the upper row begins with pin 1 on the far left and pin 13 on the right. The second row runs pins 14 through 25, again from the left to the right. The widest part of the RS-232 connector is the top (pins 1 through 13). On the Centronics connector, the widest part is the bottom (pins 1 through 18).

The best approach is to go through the entire connector, pin by pin, starting with pin 1. Mark those with no wire connected with an X. If you mark only those with wires, chances are you will lose count and end up mislabeling one or more subsequent pins.

CENTRONICS PIN GUIDE

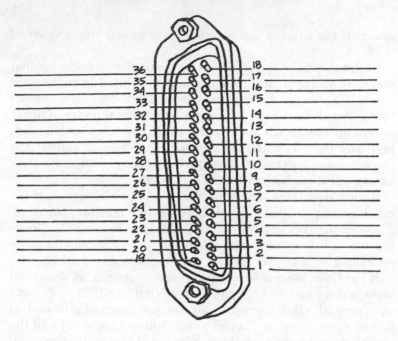

RS-232 PIN GUIDE

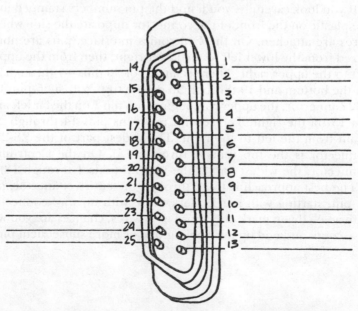

Check yourself at the end of each row to be sure your count is 18 and 36 or 13 and 25 for Centronics and RS-232, respectively.

Another major concern in tracing your connections is to be exact in describing wire colors. You'll probably have a handful of white, orange, brown, black, red, and other solid-colored wires. There also should be a few multicolored wires—white and red, white and brown, and so on. Be careful. In a poorly lit room, black and brown look a lot alike and other color combinations have a similar tendency to get mixed up. The problem's even worse with multicolored wires. It may be difficult to see the second color because, typically, the wires have white backgrounds with the second color spiraling like a snake around them. You may have to trace the wire some distance before you can see the second color. It's easy to get lost.

A basic guideline when recording the wires' colors is to assume that no two wires have the same colors. You can't absolutely count on this being true, but it's a pretty safe assumption.

When you finish with one end of the cable, go to the other. This time, start with the wires, not the pins. If pin 1 on the first end was red, find out to what pin the red wire is connected at the other end. You simply need to go down the list you made earlier.

You aren't home free yet. In many cases you'll find that, in addition to the wires running from one end to the other of a cable, there are additional wires at each end that connect one pin to another. These are known as "jumpers," so called because they "jump" an electrical circuit from one pin to another. They are used frequently to provide signals that one device needs to operate properly but which won't be sent by the other device. Your computer, for example, may need to receive a signal on RS-232 pin 5 ("Clear to Send"), but your printer may not be set up to transmit this signal. Meanwhile, your computer may be set up to transmit a signal on pin 4 ("Request to Send"). By jumping pin 4 to pin 5, your computer gets the signal it wants on pin 5, even though it is, in effect, sending it to itself.

How Wires Should Be Connected. Having eliminated the possibility of a faulty connection and bad wiring at the connector, the next step is to examine the continuity of electricity with a voltmeter or continuity tester. If pin 2 at one end is actually going to pin 2 at the other, for example, is the current getting through as it's supposed to? It generally is a good idea to check continuity on the pin or socket side of your connector, not the wire side, to be certain you aren't accidently touching other wires. See Testing Interfaces, page 116, for more on continuity testing.

If things don't check out as they should, try jiggling the wires to see if there is a loose connection or a pin not snugly in place. If you find a bad line, all is not lost; chances are good there are unused lines in your cable that can be hooked up to replace a damaged one.

Consider the logic of what happens as the result of a bad line. If your "Clear to Send" line (RS-232 pin 5) is bad, what would that do to communications? It probably would result in the printer or modem not notifying the computer that it's OK to transmit data, so nothing would ever be sent. Is that what is happening? If the problem is with a control line—pins 5, 6, and 20 on an RS-232, or pins 1, 10, 11, 12, 28, 29, and 32 on a Centronics—you may be able to temporarily jumper the lines to see if this is where your problem lies. You could wire pin 4 ("Request to Send") to pin 5 ("Clear to Send"), for example, if you are dealing with an RS-232 interface, or connect pin 1 ("Strobe") and pin 10 ("Acknowledge") on a Centronics interface if line 5 or line 10 appeared to lack continuity.

This may not always be possible. It will depend on the function of the line that appears to be bad, and in the case of the Centronics connection it will also require that logic levels match. That is, both pins must be positive or negative, not one of each.

If, having fixed bad connections or replaced bad wires, you still aren't getting the connection you need, check the logic of how various wires are connected. Is it standard? If not, you'll have to dig into the computer's and peripheral's documentation to see which wires go where and match this against what you have recorded. Don't be surprised if this shows something amiss, but double-check everything before you start unsoldering and reconnecting wires. There are often good reasons for nonstandard wiring, and you need to be sure before you go to a lot of trouble.

Parallel Interfaces. In many cases you'll find that a parallel interface cable uses only 11 lines—8 data lines, plus lines for "Strobe," "Busy," and "Chassis Ground." Some systems add the

"Acknowledge" line, and others use a full-blown implementation of the standard connecting all 36 lines. The way the interface works requires only 10 lines. "Strobe" signals your printer that the computer has put a byte of data on the line. "Busy" tells the computer when the printer, for whatever reason, cannot accept data.

This basic 11-line configuration does not allow two-way communications, but because it generally is used with printers, that's not a major problem. Also, the basic configuration doesn't directly permit the printer to signal special error conditions, such as being out of paper, or to acknowledge receipt of a character. Again, that's more a question of sophistication than of communications.

Troubleshooting Parallel Interfaces. One of the first things to look at when troubleshooting parallel interface problems is whether you are stretching the standard's length limit. Generally, a parallel interface cable can extend no farther than 6 feet. It may be possible to stretch this, but it may result in your getting no response from your printer. So, if you're violating the limit, this may be the source of the problem. The easy way to test this is to try a shorter cable to see if that clears things up.

Your next steps are similar to those used in finding problems with an RS-232 interface: Check the connections, the wiring, and the logic of the wiring.

One slight complication with the Centronics interface is that "Strobe" and "Acknowledge" are supposed to be negative. Most printer manufacturers follow this approach, but some don't. When they don't, they usually provide a switch setting or jumper option permitting you to set this up.

If all the lines check out but nothing is happening when you try to print, it may be that the polarity is reversed—a negative voltage signal at one end while the other end expects a positive voltage signal—confusing things terribly. By sending a positive signal on the "Acknowledge" line, your printer is actually telling the computer it hasn't successfully received whatever information was sent, which, depending on your software, will either put the computer on hold, waiting for a negative signal, or set up a loop in which the same character is retransmitted over and over until the computer is notified the character has been received successfully.

If a manufacturer reverses the polarity of these two lines, it is possible that the polarity of the "Strobe" and "Busy" lines are reversed, too. If your voltmeter proves this to be true, dig into the printer's documentation to find the switch setting that reverses things back to normal.

Testing Interfaces

You can buy an expensive "breakout" box that permits you to test an RS-232 circuit through LEDs (little red lights) that indicate which lines have signals. The box also permits you to quickly jumper lines to see whether this solves a problem. Breakout boxes are convenient, but they cost a lot for what is usually a one-time occurrence of setting up an interface.

You can accomplish the same thing with a multimeter—a combination voltmeter and ohmmeter—which is cheaper and has many other uses.

You have two basic choices in multimeters: analog or digital. The latter tends to be more expensive for the same set of features —roughly $45–$65 for a decent digital meter versus $25–$35 for a comparable analog. But digital multimeters seem to be popular loss leaders at places like Radio Shack and Sears, so you should be able to get a good digital multimeter on sale for around $25.

The advantages of digital over analog are that digital is easier to read and generally more sensitive. Multimeters are rated according to their "input sensitivity," expressed in ohms per volt. The higher the rating, the better, although anything above 30 megohms is overkill. Look also at the ranges provided. With your computer, you'll be measuring DC voltages ranging from about 1 volt to 20 volts and AC voltage of 120 volts.

In reading voltages with a multimeter, a voltage must be measured with reference to something else. Generally, you will be reading voltages at some place in a circuit with the reference point being ground. If you move your ground lead from chassis ground, you will most likely get a very different reading.

When you test continuity in a circuit, a short circuit will read at or near 0 ohms resistance, while an open circuit—one with no continuity—will give an infinite reading.

Where's the Data? One of the most common problems you'll encounter with an RS-232 circuit is having both operating devices configured as if they were computers or peripherals. Often, all that you must do to solve this is to switch lines 2 and 3.

To begin, leave the cable connected to your computer. When an RS-232 circuit is idle, line 2 from the computer should be at a negative voltage, somewhere between −5 volts and −15 volts. Test this by attaching the voltmeter's negative probe to line 2 and the positive probe to line 7 (which provides the reference voltage for the various signals). If line 2 is set up to transmit data, it should give you a voltage reading of between −5 and −15.

Now test pin 3. Because this line is used for communications to the computer, it should give a positive reading. Connect your positive probe to pin 3 and the negative to pin 7. Is the voltage reading between +5 and +15? If so, you have established that your computer is correctly configured.

Now reverse the process. Pull the cable off the computer and attach it to the printer or modem. You should get a positive reading on line 2 and a negative one on line 3. If this happens, your printer or modem is correctly configured and your problem lies elsewhere. If it is not happening, both the computer and the printer probably are trying to transmit on pin 2 and receive on pin 3. To correct this, switch line 2 from the computer to line 3 on the printer or modem, and line 3 from the computer to line 2 at the other end. This may not totally solve your problem, however, because the required handshaking also will be reversed. The solution here is some clever jumpering of lines—most likely line 4 to line 5, and possibly lines 8 and 20 to 6, or some combination of these. (See the common RS-232 configuration illustrations for some typical examples.)

Additional Tests. If the computer doesn't appear to be transmitting data, you can test the cable's configuration by unplugging the printer or modem and testing line 2. Data will register about −5 to −15 volts. If you hook the negative probe to pin 2 and the positive probe to pin 7 and send data from the computer, you should see the voltmeter needle vibrate. At higher baud rates, this vibration may be imperceptible, so you should set the baud rate as low as you can.

7
KEYBOARDS

The keyboard is the main link between you and your computer. While there are a growing number of other ways to communicate with your computer—among them the joystick, the mouse, and, increasingly, your voice—the old reliable QWERTY keyboard remains the input device of choice for most computer users.

Basically, a keyboard is a collection of switches. When you press a key, you "turn on" a switch, sending a signal that identifies the key you hit. Then circuitry in the keyboard or the computer translates the signal into an instruction—to print a character on the screen, to return to the next line, to delete a character, or whatever. That's all there is to it. Computer manufacturers have developed a number of switching mechanisms for keyboards, but when you examine each closely, you'll see that each does the same thing: translates your fingers' movements into instructions.

On the outside, however, one keyboard can look very different from another. One major difference is between typewriter-style keyboards and membrane keyboards. You already know about the common typewriter-style keyboards—the ones with keys that rise individually from the keyboard and, as you press and release them, spring back up. Membrane keyboards don't have individual keys. Instead, there is a single plastic sheet with the layout of the keys printed on it. Under the plastic sheet there are—what else?—rows of switches that generate a signal for a particular key.

On most typewriter-style keyboards, you can pry off the individual key tops and find the underlying switches. Under each key top, you'll usually find a rod, plunger, or similar device which, when pressed, completes a circuit or otherwise generates an electrical signal. The plunger sits on or rides through a spring, which is responsible for making the key pop up after you release it.

The key housing is mounted on a circuit board with two or more prongs, which are soldered in place. These, in turn, are tied to a number of circuit lines that carry the signals from keys to computer.

ANATOMY OF A KEY

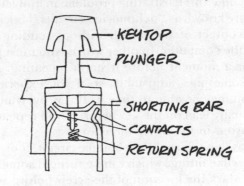

KEYTOP
PLUNGER
SHORTING BAR
CONTACTS
RETURN SPRING

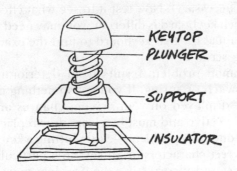

KEYTOP
PLUNGER
SUPPORT
INSULATOR

Signs of Trouble

Given the mechanical nature of keyboards, it is surprising how reliable and long-lasting they are. Failures, when they occur, generally result from worn-out switch contacts or springs—or plain old abuse.

Typewriter-style mechanical switches tend to have "bouncing" problems. Many keyboards are designed to repeat a key if you hold the key down for a second or two. Sometimes, however, hitting the key just once causes repeated generation of the key signal, resulting in some or all characters being rreeeppeeeaattteeedd several times.

To overcome this frustrating problem, manufacturers incorporate what are known as "debouncing circuits." Such circuits allow for extra contact of the switch without sending multiple keystrokes to the computer. In other words, you must press and hold the key for a moment before it starts repeating. A debouncing circuit is sometimes adjustable, so if you experience excessive bounce you may be able to tune it. If it is overtuned—requiring you to virtually lean on the key before it will repeat—it may need to be adjusted in the other direction.

If you have an adjustable debounce circuit, look for something with a screwlike fitting, which can be turned, somewhere on your keyboard. Mark the location of the screw before you change the setting, then give it a half turn in one direction or the other (again, make a note on what you are doing so you can easily adjust it back if necessary). Now test it to see what effect this has had. Because each keyboard is different, you may need to consult the technical manual for that keyboard to find the exact location of the adjusting screw.

Another common problem results from deterioration of an individual key switch or spring. If you get something other than the key you hit displayed on your screen, chances are the key switch itself is defective and must be cleaned or replaced. If you have more than one such problem—either hitting a key generates a series of incorrect characters or all keys in a particular area of the keyboard respond incorrectly—the problem more likely involves one of the circuit lines on the back of the keyboard.

Preventing Problems

The greatest threats to your keyboard are the spaghetti, Pepsi, and assorted other foods computer-types have a tendency to pour on their equipment, which are joined by the ambient dust, grime, and goop that normally accumulates on just about anything electronic. Newer keyboards are designed in such a way that key tops fit over their switch housings, limiting the amount of debris that can get inside. The membrane-style keyboards are rather hardy in this respect. The original IBM PCjr keyboard, for example, contains rubber suction cups under each key. The cups are fixed onto a layer of rubber that guards the keyboard wiring underneath. The wiring itself is inside another protective layer, effectively sealing off the electrical contacts. You can virtually take it swimming, but don't do this. (See also The Dishwasher Solution, page 122.)

For those with more vulnerable keyboards, keeping food and other contaminants away is the key to keyboard longevity. If you need convincing, take an iron nail and put it in a bottle of cola for twenty-four hours. That carbon dioxide fizz in your favorite soft drink, when mixed with water, forms a mild acid that just loves to eat up metal—including the springs, rods, and assorted electrical components that live inside your computer. If you really gum things up with spilled liquids or other sticky stuff, you may have to use alcohol or electrical-contact/relay cleaner to clean things up. (See We'll Drink to That, page 26.)

Getting dust and other loose matter out of a keyboard is simple: Simply turn the board upside down and blow it out with a reversed vacuum cleaner. (Do it as far away as possible from the rest of your computer.)

Solving Problems

What you can do to solve keyboard problems depends largely on the type of keyboard and the type of problem. Generally, if you have a membrane-type keyboard, there isn't much you can do

The Dishwasher Solution

Technical engineers are frequently called into offices to fix bad keyboards. No one ever seems to know what happened to the board—it just stopped working. But a quick examination reveals the telltale sticky liquid that had been someone's lunch just before it mysteriously ended up among the vowels, consonants, and punctuation marks.

There are ways to clean circuit boards that involve bathing the component in various liquids, similar to those the boards are put through after they are originally soldered. But this is relatively expensive because the keyboard usually must be sent to a factory or service depot for this procedure.

One innovative and daring service engineer we know found a quicker, cheaper solution. He simply takes the abused board home and runs it through his dishwasher, using the highest-temperature drying cycle.

We can't find this technique mentioned in any service manual and, therefore, are somewhat reluctant to recommend it. But it works, says our friend. The trick is to be certain that the unit is dried completely to prevent rusting. Thoroughly inspect all wiring to be sure none was damaged in the process.

If the choice is to buy a new keyboard or spend a small fortune to have yours cleaned, you've got nothing to lose in trying the dishwasher solution. But easy Duz it.

to fix it. The underlying circuitry is a single unit; if you have a problem with an individual key, the entire keypad may need replacing.

Sticking Keys. If you have a key that sticks or is difficult to press, you may be able to replace the spring if it is exposed when you remove the key top. If the spring is built into the key, you'll have to replace the entire key. This is relatively simple, even though it involves desoldering and resoldering the contacts. Unlike other desoldering/resoldering jobs, you generally have plenty of room to work and there isn't much heat-sensitive circuitry or other components to worry about. You still must be careful, of course, avoiding dropping solder where it doesn't belong, which can cause a short circuit. Otherwise, even a relative novice should be able to tackle a keyboard solder job successfully.

Lubricants won't solve sticking-key difficulties because the problem is likely to be either dirt or a bad spring. Squirting lubricants on the keyboard just provides the keyboard with a sticky material that attracts more dirt and grime. A shot of electrical-contact/relay cleaner or even rubbing alcohol may help, but try this only after exhausting other methods.

Bad Switches. Before you undertake a desoldering/resoldering job on a bad switch, make sure the problem isn't simply a bad solder contact on the original soldered connection. Often one or more contacts of a key switch have a bad connection—perhaps it came loose from all that pressing. Poke around to see if there is any loose solder, then try heating the solder to see if this fixes it. If it doesn't, desolder the contact, clean it up, and then resolder it.

If there is no obvious solder problem, chances are something within the switch itself is bad. There's a chance you can fix this by taking apart a typewriter-style key switch, bending the contacts, and cleaning it out. Usually, however, this won't do much good, but it's still worth trying before you fire up the soldering iron or take the machine to a technician.

The integrated plastic housing of modern keyboard switches doesn't allow you much chance to get inside to correct problems. This is the price you pay for the added protection such switches provide against soft drinks and assorted other goop. If this is the case with your keyboard, you'll have to replace the entire key.

The Right Key. Finding a key to replace a bad one isn't always an easy task. Few computer stores and service centers carry keys. Your best bet is to approach an independent electronics store that carries components to see if it can obtain a key for you. Be nice. Ordering a single key, unless it is readily available from a distributor, probably won't be high on its list of things to do. You may, in fact, have to settle for suggestions about where you can

GOOD VS. BAD SOLDER POINTS

GOOD

BAD

get a replacement key, then continue the search until you achieve success.

Another avenue for obtaining a replacement key may be a local users' group or bulletin board. Chances are you won't actually locate a key from such sources, but you may locate an old keyboard you can cannibalize or one that came with the original machine but which has been replaced by an aftermarket board that offers a better layout or other enhancement. (These are popular among IBM PC owners, many of whom dislike, to put it nicely, the original IBM PC keyboard. A small industry of aftermarket keyboards was created as a result. Meanwhile, the original, detested keyboard is typically relegated to some closet shelf. The same is true with the IBM PCjr "Chiclet"-style keyboard.) You should be able to pick up an old keyboard for a song, if not for free.

Depending on the type of keyboard you have, you may be able to get by with any old key switch (keyboards on which any key switch can be interchanged with any other key switch) or you may need a specific key (keyboards on which each key switch is different). Determining which type you have may involve checking a technical manual or asking some knowledgeable person at a computer store, users' group, or electronic bulletin board.

The main problem you'll encounter with your keyboard is getting it dirty, and, as we said earlier, the solution is to keep it clean. There's no way around this.

8
MODEMS

Modems are very useful devices. If you want to get in touch with one of the information data bases—CompuServe or The Source, for example—you need a modem. A modem also provides you with a wonderful link to information about problems you may be having with your computer equipment or software through the countless homegrown electronic bulletin boards that have sprung up in communities large and small.

The good news is that modems are incredibly reliable, without any moving parts. Once operating properly, there is little that can go awry. The bad news is that, modem reliability notwithstanding, data communications between computers can be one of the most frustrating experiences in all personal computerdom. The reason has a lot to do with the precise connections that must be made between modems, computers, and telephones and the wide range of communication protocols upon which two communicating computers must agree before data will be transmitted successfully. To solve such problems requires a bit of understanding of how modems and data communications work.

Modems come in a variety of sizes, shapes, models, and colors, but the most important difference is in the speed at which they operate—the baud rate. Baud is the number of bits transmitted per second. Most modems range between 300 and 9,600 baud, although several companies are working on new systems that permit transmission at 56,000 baud—that's more than 5,000 characters per second. (Baud rate can be translated roughly to characters per second by dividing the rate by 10.)

Modems take the relatively weak digital signals from your computer and convert them to signals that fit the characteristics of the telephone system. The technical details aren't important. Suffice it to say that modems use different techniques to transfer information over phone lines, and the principal differences vary according to the speed of transmission. A 300-baud modem uses a different technique for communicating than does a 1,200-baud modem; the differences continue as speed increases.

Once upon a time, anything attached to a phone line was produced by Ma Bell. Later, after years of court and legislative attack, devices made by other companies were permitted to be attached to the phone system. Included in that category were modems, which were just becoming a popular tool among computer-types. Anything that was attached, however, had to meet Ma Bell's standards.

The two standards relating to most modems are known as Bell 103 and Bell 212, representing the worlds of 300 and 1,200 baud, respectively. Again, the technical differences aren't important. What's important to know is that a Bell 103 modem can communicate only with another 103 modem. The 212 standard, however, requires that a 212 modem also be a 103 modem, so a 212 can talk with both another 212 modem and a 103 modem. (A 103 modem can talk to a 212 modem, but only at 300 baud, not at 1,200.)

With changes in the national telephone system—most notably the new circuit-switched digital-capability system—personal computer owners may be treated to low-cost, high-speed data communications in the near future. This will mean not only greater speed, but also greater accuracy in data transmission.

The Odds of Getting Even

It may seem a contradiction to state that higher speed equals greater accuracy, but it's true. There are two factors at work that lower error rates at higher speeds. The first is that higher-speed communication uses more sophisticated techniques for transmitting data. This in itself reduces errors. The second reason is that with higher speeds it's possible to use more sophisticated error-checking-and-correcting techniques.

The simplest form of error checking is known as "parity checking." There are three kinds of parity: even, odd, or none. The choice is up to the communicating parties; it doesn't matter which you choose, as long as both parties use the same parity. How parity checking works is pretty straightforward. Every character you transmit—letters (both upper and lower case), numbers, punctuation, special symbols, carriage returns, and on and on—is in your computer as a series of "0s" and "1s." In each character, there is either an even or an odd number of "1s." The computer counts the number of "1s" in each individual character (for example, the ASCII code for the letter e—1100001—has three "1s"). So when you transmit data using "even parity," if the total is not an even number, an additional "1"—the parity bit—is added to produce an even number. If the character already has an even number of "1s," a "0" is added as the parity bit. When using even parity, the receiving computer expects to get an even number of "1s" with each character. If it doesn't, it signifies an error in transmission, known as a "parity error."

There are real problems with parity as an error-checking scheme. If you have two errors, they can cancel each other out and slide by undetected. Fortunately, this doesn't happen often. When there's a problem on a phone line, it tends to affect a whole string of characters, not just a bit or two. When lightning strikes, it zaps a number of bits. The same generally is true of other disturbances that affect phone lines.

At higher speeds, more sophisticated techniques are used, both to flag errors and to correct them. These same techniques can be used at lower speeds, but they generally are not worth the hassle.

Some error-checking-and-correcting procedures send data in blocks. At the end of each block, some statistic describing the block is transmitted. In some ways this isn't much different from parity error checking except that the statistic describes a whole block of data rather than a single character. One such popular technique is known as "XMODEM," or "Ward Christensen protocol." A block of 128 characters is sent along with a statistic, which is computed by looking at all the "0s" and "1s" in the entire block. The receiving computer calculates this same number, and if the two match, it tells the sending machine to go ahead with the next block. If there is a discrepancy, the receiving machine says so and the block is retransmitted.

Error-checking-and-correcting routines can be very sophisticated and are absolutely necessary when you send something like a program over the phone. With text, parity checking may suffice because, in many cases, you can correct an error just by examining the text. The error then can be corrected manually by the recipient. When you send a compiled program (as opposed to the text listing of a program), you have to get everything right; there's virtually no way to determine what got missent.

How Modems Differ

For all practical purposes, a Bell 103 modem is a Bell 103 modem. Having said that, there can be any number of differences between two Bell 103 modems. To start, there are devices known as "acoustic couplers." They are just like any other modem except that they aren't connected directly to a phone line. Instead, you place the telephone handset into two cushioned cups. As the name implies, "direct-connect" modems hook directly to a phone line using a standard modular telephone jack.

Beyond these basic differences, there are a number of bells and whistles that can be built into any modem. A modem can be set up to dial a number automatically, for example, rather than you having to dial the number yourself. It can have pulse dialing or Touch-tone dialing. It can be set up to automatically answer calls, or you may have to do this manually. It may have a number of "status lights" telling you whether it is sending or receiving or any number of other things. A modem may not even be visible (at least not with your computer's cover on)—it may be built into your computer, rather than existing as a separate device. The list goes on.

At the heart of a modem is the circuitry that prepares an electrical signal for transmission over a phone line or takes a signal from a phone line and converts it to one your computer can use.

Normally, the greater the complexity of a device, the greater the chance of problems. This is not necessarily the case with modems. Most principal circuits in today's modems are available in standard integrated-circuit chips. There are even entire modems on a chip. Because such integrated circuits require less power and fewer soldered connections, this means greater reliability.

What Can Go Wrong

Data communications is without a doubt one of the trickiest things you'll ever do with a computer. It isn't that it is particularly difficult; it's just that there are so many things that can go wrong. If you have problems getting a modem set up or communicating once you have things going, you would do well to read Chapter 6 on interfaces.

One thing you can count on with modems: If you have a problem, it isn't likely to be a difficulty with the hardware. You should write this on a piece of paper and tape it on or near your modem to save yourself a lot of anxiety and frustration. When you're having trouble communicating between two computers, chances are overwhelming that something is amiss with switch settings or cabling or that there is a mismatch between the two computers' software. It's probably not a breakdown of a computer or modem. The chances of a hardware failure are so small it isn't worth investigating, at least not until everything else has been checked, double-checked, and ruled out.

In the arcane world of data communications, a computer is known as a "data terminal" and a modem as a "data set." They are known also as DTEs (data terminal equipment) and DCEs (data communications equipment), respectively. Straightforward enough, right? Wrong!

The problem goes back to the old days, before microcomputers. Big mainframe computers and their high priests in the computer room made the rules. Out there in the boonies among lowly "end users" were some miserable pieces of equipment called "terminals" (also known, predictably, as "dumb terminals"), which communicated with a central computer using a modem. Hence the terms DTE and DCE.

Things really became messy when minicomputers made the scene. These were real live computers in their own right. One computer must be a DTE, the high priests decided, and the other a DCE. There's no way around it; you must have one of each or you can't communicate. But the high priests weren't about to allow these little minicomputers to call themselves "computers," a term reserved for the behemoth mainframe beasts that consumed mass quantities of electricity, air-conditioning, and human resources.

So you had this weird setup, with terminals, set up as DTEs, wired to minicomputers, which, in turn, were wired to mainframes, also set up as DTEs. The result: confusion. The confusion has carried over to the world of micros.

Why does all this matter? It seems that an outdated argument in semantics would be of little or no relevance to today's sophisticated world of computing. But no. Such notions determine which machine gets to talk on which line when the two are connected.

An RS-232 connection is almost always used between a computer and a modem. If a computer manufacturer has chosen to configure its product as a communications device (DCE), there will be problems if it tries to communicate with a modem set up as a DCE. Under the rules of RS-232, a computer (or DTE) transmits on line 2 (of the 25 potential lines in an RS-232 cable) and receives on line 3. A modem (or DCE), on the other hand, is set up to receive on line 2 and transmit on line 3. If both machines are set up as DCEs, the resulting conflict is obvious. (For more on RS-232, see Chapter 6 on interfaces.)

Null Modems

As you can see from the above, you can run into problems right from the start in data communications. Before your computer can communicate with the world, you must get your computer communicating with your modem.

The most common problem you'll encounter in this first stage is having a computer that is configured by its manufacturer as a modem. Some modem manufacturers anticipated such problems and provide a switch that allows you to reconfigure your modem by changing switch settings, rather than by getting a special cable.

If your computer's RS-232 port is set up as a modem and your modem can't be reconfigured, the solution is simply to reverse two or more lines in the cable that connects the two. (See Chapter 6 for details on null modems.)

Setting Switches

Modems, like printers, usually come with several banks of dip switches. These switches are necessary so that a standard modem can be hooked up to the wide variety of computers on the market, each with its own unique interpretation of what constitutes an RS-232 connection. The problems here go well beyond the question of which machine talks on which line and listens on which line. (For reasons known only to a spirit buried deep in corporate engineering departments, most computer manufacturers have chosen a nonstandard implementation of RS-232. Not only do they change and intermix the direction of some signals, they put certain signals on lines on which they simply don't belong.)

This is why modem (and printer) manufacturers have been forced to load their machines with banks of switches. It is the only way to permit one machine to be connected with many different computers. Fortunately, printer and modem manufacturers have become very good at providing information on what settings are appropriate for each machine, so you should be able to find the information you need readily in a modem's instruction manual or by calling one of the modem manufacturer's technical whiz kids.

If you have chosen not to use the standard serial port that comes with your computer, using instead a port contained on an add-on board, you'll have to patiently match the pin configurations at each end as well as provide appropriate cabling. There is nothing particularly difficult about this. You just need to be sure you have set everything up as it should be, then double-check all settings and cable pin assignments.

Note that many of the assignments you make by setting switches on your modem or serial board can be overridden by your communications software. You'll probably have a baud rate selection option, for example, as well as a word size switch (the number of data bits per byte) and other settings. Setting these at a particular rate or size may do nothing more than provide a default setting that your software can override by sending appropriate control signals.

The greatest difficulty you may face is pinning down a problem. Long after you have successfully set everything up and have become a telecommunications ace—skipping around the public phone network from bulletin board to data base to electronic mail system—you'll still run into communications problems. Worse yet, it will be extremely difficult to tell whether you have a computer-to-modem cabling problem, a switch-setting problem, or a software problem—or even whether the problem actually has to do with the computer with which you're trying to communicate.

To start, it will help to know the six basic parameters involved in telecommunications:

* speed, or baud rate
* word size, or number of data bits per byte
* parity
* number of stop bits
* flow control
* error-checking-and-correcting protocol

Let's take them one at a time.

Speed. For the most part, you will be limited to either 300 baud or 1,200 baud, depending on whether you have a Bell 103 or Bell 212 modem. Both computers must operate at the same speed to avoid what are known as framing errors. If your computer is sending data at 300 baud and the other person's computer thinks data is coming in at 1,200 baud, the result will be what is commonly known as "garbage."

Word Size. Similarly, if your computer assumes a character is seven bits long but the other computer expects to receive eight-bit–long characters, the one-bit difference will render your computer's data unintelligible.

Parity. Parity must also be matched. Depending on your software, an incoming character perceived by the receiving computer to be an error itself may be preserved intact, or a parity error "flag"—a question mark, for example—may be substituted for the character that failed the parity test.

Stop Bits. Generally, you should always use one stop bit. In the days of 110-baud Teletype machines, one-and-a-half, two, and two-and-a-half stop bits often were required. Today, one stop bit is enough, but you usually still have the option to set this to two. Without agreement on the number of bits, you'll end up with what amounts to a framing error. If you send ten bits and the other computer reads a character as nine bits, you aren't going to do much communicating.

Flow Control. This can be devilish. Flow control enables the receiving machine to tell the transmitting computer to stop sending. Perhaps it needs a break to write information from memory to disk (even computers get bogged down) or has some other housekeeping chore to attend to. The two machines must agree in advance how to handle this. The most common form of flow control is known as "X-ON/X-OFF." When your computer, the receiving machine, needs a break, it sends the other computer an "X-OFF" character (ASCII DC3, also known as "Control S," with the decimal value 19 and the hexidecimal value 13). As soon as the other computer sees this, it stops sending until it gets an "X-ON" character (ASCII DC1, also known as "Control Q," with the decimal value 17 and the hex value 11). That's convention, but some computer-types decided to substitute other values for the "X-ON/X-OFF" characters. So, the characters can be any of the first 32 ASCII characters. You also may use some of the possible combinations that have decimal values between 128 and 256, which can be created using eight bits but which fall outside the standard ASCII code set. (See the ASCII table on page 138 for the possible characters that may be used as flow control signals.)

Another common approach to flow control involves two other sets of ASCII control characters: "Carriage Return (CR)/Line Feed (LF)" (decimal 13, hex 0D and decimal 10, hex 0A, respectively) or "Acknowledge (ACK)/Negative Acknowledge (NAK)" (decimal 6, hex 6 and decimal 21, hex 15, respectively). In the first case, the transmitting machine sends a line of characters, typically a line of text or eighty characters (a throwback to the days of eighty-column punch cards). It then sends a carriage return and waits for a line feed from the receiving computer to let it know it's OK to send the next batch of data. With "ACK/NAK," the receiving machine sends an "ACK" after receiving a block of data if it's ready to receive more. If it needs a break, it sends a "NAK," goes about its housekeeping business, and sends an "ACK" when ready to resume. The transmitting machine also may send an "End of Text" (ETX) control character (decimal 3 and hex 03) at the end of each block of data and wait for an "ACK" before resuming transmission.

Don't put it past software developers to devise other schemes, including combinations of the above, for flow-control systems.

If the two computers aren't together on flow control, the whole process of communications can come to an abrupt end. If nothing happens from the start, or if you get a single block of data and everything stops, the problem probably lies in matching the flow-control scheme between the two machines.

Error Checking and Correcting. There are a number of error-checking-and-correcting protocols on the market. The "XMODEM," or "Ward Christensen protocol," has gained relatively wide acceptance, but, as usual, there are a number of dialects with which you must deal. Manufacturers of modems and communications software have developed their own proprietary schemes based on the (usually false) assumption that eventually everyone will be using their machine or software.

Typically, such routines involve transmitting a block of data along with some statistics that are mathematically derived from the data, much like even or odd parity is calculated from the individual characteristics of the data bits in a byte. The differences are that error checking uses much more complex mathematical calculations and that the result is derived from a large block of data instead of a single byte.

When the block of data and its accompanying statistic are sent, the transmitting machine waits for the receiving machine to let it know that the block was received correctly. If it was, the sender fires off the next block. If there was a problem, the original block must be re-sent. This continues until the data are sent without error or, if the errors continue time after time, until some preset number of unsuccessful tries is reached.

The problems aren't over. Even after you have hardware and software properly configured for communications, you'll still run into problems beyond the control of a mere mortal, even one armed to the teeth with state-of-the-art testing gear.

If you pick up a telephone, for example, you are likely to hear a little static every once in a while. During a storm, the static can be particularly bad. It also can be bad in some parts of a city but not in others. Moreover, your house or office may have other machines connected to your phone lines—or may have plain bad wiring—which can wreak additional havoc on computer telecommunications. Many such problems are unexplainable and unpredictable, with good reason: They are the results of electronic ghosts, gremlins, and glitches.

The more you telecommunicate, the more likely you are to believe in such phenomena. Sometimes you must simply hang up and redial. Or you may have to wait for the ghost, gremlin, or glitch to pass before you can communicate without errors. But don't jump to the conclusion that solving a problem is out of your hands. Chances are good you are the culprit. Check the settings.

Prevention and Repair

Once you have set up a modem and it has worked for a while, it should keep going for a long time. The reason: More and more of the modem's circuitry is being crammed into one highly reliable integrated-circuit chip.

The most vulnerable part of a modem is the power supply, usually consisting of a transformer that decreases 120-volt AC household current to 12 volts or less DC. A lot of heat is dissipated in this process, and, over time, this circuitry can break down. In most cases, the electrical conversion occurs in a little unit that you plug into the wall. The only direct contact your modem has with the transformer is via a wire from the transformer, so damage is restricted to the transformer itself.

Beyond the power supply, most other circuitry runs on low

voltages and isn't subject to problems. Because the modem tends to be a self-contained unit, dust and dirt shouldn't be problems.

If your modem is built into the computer on a separate board or the main circuit board, you may have to clean it periodically to keep it from getting overrun with dust and other gunk. If it is a plug-in board, it may become unseated, and you may have to pull the board, clean the contacts, and reseat it every once in a while. That's about it. There may be an electronic component or two that will burn out, especially if the modem's power supply is built into the unit. In such cases, heat may affect a weak component, resulting in its breaking down after the modem has been on for a while. This can happen if the modem is kept in a poorly ventilated place. The symptoms you'll notice will be erratic behavior or a complete shutdown. (See Chapter 4 on the central processor.) But before you go to the trouble of tearing a modem apart, check its connections and make sure it is properly configured.

It's very useful to find a bulletin board or a friend with whom you know you have no problem communicating. When things don't seem to be working properly, try communicating with Old Reliable and see what happens. To make this a relatively goof-proof test, set up a special disk with the appropriate software—one that isn't used on a daily basis—to help determine whether you have a software problem.

Status Symbols and Self-Tests

Years ago computers had all kinds of flashing lights on their front panels. With the relative unreliability of computer circuits, these lights were vital for monitoring a computer and tracing down malfunctions. Many modem manufacturers still provide a panel of LEDs (light-emitting diodes—those little red lights) that indicate the status of the modem, whether it's connected to the computer, and the flow of data out of the computer and over the phone.

The reason for such lights today isn't the unreliability of the modem but the need for some sort of visual signal as a clue to what is happening when things aren't working properly. If you are sending and your modem "Send" (SD) light isn't blinking, you may have a clue to the problem.

If your modem has status lights, it also may have built-in self-testing circuitry. These circuits permit a variety of tests to be performed, ranging from an internal check of the modem to an over-the-phone test of a remote connection. The variations on this theme are quite wide. Some manufacturers provide nothing. Others give you a whole range of tests. You'll have to check your modem's owner's manual.

It's worth repeating: When you have a telecommunications problem, chances are extremely high that it isn't the modem. Instead:

* Check the physical connections to be sure they are solid.
* Check the cable configuration and switch settings.
* Make sure you have selected the appropriate communications parameters.

Only after doing this—and double-checking everything—should you consider a modem failure as the source of your problem.

The ASCII Character Chart

Decimal	Hex	ASCII	Decimal	Hex	ASCII
0	00	NUL	15	0F	SI
1	01	SOH	16	10	DLE
2	02	STX	17	11	DC1
3	03	ETX	18	12	DC2
4	04	EOT	19	13	DC3
5	05	ENQ	20	14	DC4
6	06	ACK	21	15	NAK
7	07	BEL	22	16	SYN
8	08	BS	23	17	ETB
9	09	HT	24	18	CAN
10	0A	LF	25	19	EM
11	0B	VT	26	1A	SUB
12	0C	FF	27	1B	ESC
13	0D	CR	28	1C	FS
14	0E	SO	29	1D	GS

30	1E	RS	69	45	E
31	1F	US	70	46	F
32	20	SP	71	47	G
33	21	!	72	48	H
34	22	"	73	49	I
35	23	#	74	4A	J
36	24	$	75	4B	K
37	25	%	76	4C	L
38	26	&	77	4D	M
39	27	'	78	4E	N
40	28	(	79	4F	O
41	29	)	80	50	P
42	2A	*	81	51	Q
43	2B	+	82	52	R
44	2C	,	83	53	S
45	2D	-	84	54	T
46	2E	.	85	55	U
47	2F	/	86	56	V
48	30	0	87	57	W
49	31	1	88	58	X
50	32	2	89	59	Y
51	33	3	90	5A	Z
52	34	4	91	5B	[
53	35	5	92	5C	\
54	36	6	93	5D	]
55	37	7	94	5E	^
56	38	8	95	5F	—
57	39	9	96	60	`
58	3A	:	97	61	a
59	3B	;	98	62	b
60	3C	<	99	63	c
61	3D	=	100	64	d
62	3E	>	101	65	e
63	3F	?	102	66	f
64	40	@	103	67	g
65	41	A	104	68	h
66	42	B	105	69	i
67	43	C	106	6A	j
68	44	D	107	6B	k

Decimal	Hex	ASCII	Decimal	Hex	ASCII
108	6C	l	118	76	v
109	6D	m	119	77	w
110	6E	n	120	78	x
111	6F	o	121	79	y
112	70	p	122	7A	z
113	71	q	123	7B	{
114	72	r	124	7C		
115	73	s	125	7D	}
116	74	t	126	7E	-
117	75	u	127	7F	DEL

9
MONITORS

Computer monitors come in a variety of shapes and sizes and include cathode ray tubes (CRTs), which resemble ordinary television sets, and liquid crystal displays (LCDs), which typically have dark characters and a light background, appearing like the squarish numbers often found in calculators. There are a few other exotic forms of monitors, such as plasma displays, but they haven't yet become widely accepted in the world of personal computers.

CRTs may be either monochrome (one color)—white letters on a black background, black letters on white, amber on black, green on black, and so on—or in color, with a range of 4, 6, 8, or 16 primary color choices. Some personal computer owners use ordinary television sets with their computers, while others choose high-resolution monitors designed specifically for computers.

LCD displays, typical of calculators and lap-size computers, usually provide black characters on silver or white, although the colors may be reversed. The first computers with LCD monitors had only one-row displays of forty or fewer characters. Today, LCD displays with twenty-four rows of eighty characters are common. Several firms are hard at work developing color LCD displays.

The major advantage of CRTs over LCDs is that CRTs can more quickly change from one display to another. One other advantage is that the screen can be viewed from almost any angle; LCDs usually must be viewed straight on.

LCDs, on the other hand, consume very little electricity compared with CRTs, making them suitable for portable, battery-powered computers. At first, the quality of characters displayed on the screen was limited to the familiar seven-segment shape of numbers appearing on your digital watch or pocket calculator. This has improved dramatically in recent years, and even better character quality is coming.

Both types of monitors are among the more reliable parts of a computer system. There's a good chance your monitor can provide trouble-free service for years, assuming a few preventive maintenance tasks (see Chapter 3).

Cathode Ray Tubes

First, a few important words: Messing around with a cathode ray tube can be quite hazardous. We highly recommend that you not attempt any repairs on or adjustments to the CRT directly. If other circuitry of your computer is located in the same cabinet as the CRT, proceed with great caution to avoid inadvertently getting a severe electrical shock.

A cathode ray tube contains a source of electrons and a phosphor-coated screen within a specially designed vacuum tube. Under high voltage, electrons are emitted by the electron gun, or cathode, and accelerated toward the screen. The gun scans the screen at a predetermined rate—say, sixty-five times per second —and projects electrons according to an electronic signal. When the electrons interact with the screen's phosphor coating, light is produced and an image is displayed.

In a computer, a character to be displayed is stored in memory. The character then goes to another section of memory, where information on the pattern necessary to display the character is located. From there it passes to circuitry that generates the appropriate signals to fire off the correct pattern in the proper location on your screen. On the CRT itself are a number of adjustments required to keep the display in focus, properly aligned on the screen, and so on.

As we said earlier, we recommend that you *not* attempt any adjustment of a CRT unless there are external knobs that permit this.

Making appropriate adjustments to a CRT is a fairly straightforward process, but it must be weighed against the possibility of getting a high-voltage shock. Most adjustments are best made when the power is on, when voltages can be upward of 10,000 volts. Such a jolt might not kill you, but it probably would knock your socks off and make you consider updating your last will and testament.

If you understand nothing else, understand this: *A CRT can store a high-voltage charge even when the power is off.* You must be very careful when working around a CRT, particularly with computers such as the TRS-80 and any of the portables that have a CRT and other circuitry housed in the same cabinet. Just because the machine is turned off and unplugged doesn't mean that you won't get a surge of electrons charging through your body looking for ground.

The risks of doing it yourself are simply too large when you consider that you can replace most monitors for about $100 to $200. There is simply no reason to take a chance that you can fix a CRT without getting a shock when the cost of replacing it, or having it adjusted professionally, is so low.

Liquid Crystal Displays

The voltages involved in LCDs are so low that you can safely play around with these if you encounter a problem. An LCD works by electronically charging an area, forcing the liquid crystal material to align itself so that it blocks the passage of light, thereby forming the patterns on your screen. The remaining uncharged area continues to be translucent, allowing light to pass through and be reflected back.

Unlike a CRT, an LCD requires a large amount of wiring so that each picture element can be turned on and off. The major problems you'll encounter with an LCD is with this wiring.

What You Can and Can't Do

The main problems with CRTs are very similar to those you'll encounter with television sets: the display isn't properly centered

We Interrupt
This Program . . .

The scenario goes something like this: It's a quiet evening around the house. Everyone else is watching TV, but you'd rather play with your computer. You sit down at your machine, turn it on, and the noise begins. No, it's not from your computer—it's from your family, complaining that your computer is causing the TV picture to become snowy.

The problem is radio frequency interference, or RFI, radio waves transmitted by your computer and by many other electronic devices. A computer's RFI is supposed to be shielded by the housing of the computer itself, but at times some RFI escapes. When it does, your computer acts as something of a broadcast transmitter, beaming RFI to nearby antennas, including those attached to nearby televisions. The result: Although it's August, there's a blizzard on your TV screen.

Often the interference comes from a poorly grounded machine. It may come from the monitor itself or any of its com-

or is out of focus or distorted, especially on the outer edges. You shouldn't attempt to correct such problems yourself, however, unless you are familiar with working on CRTs.

Problems unique to computer monitors have to do with the circuits that generate the characters on the screen. If you look closely at your monitor, you'll see that each character is made up of a number of dots or short lines (known as "pixels" or "rasters"). The pattern for each character is typically stored in your computer's permanent read-only memory (ROM). If you find that a particular character is usually out of whack, it is likely that the problem is in the character ROM, which you'll have to replace.

The other kind of problem typical of computer CRTs is constantly having a blank or otherwise messed-up area of your screen. This, too, is a memory problem—in this case, the screen ponents. Foolproof solutions to control RFI are expensive. You'd need a power-line filter/regulator, for example, which reduces most of the emissions, or additional shielding of the computer, monitor, and all cables. Such solutions can cost upward of a couple hundred dollars.

A few simple tricks can help you identify the RFI culprit and minimize or eliminate the problems. Among the things worth trying are the following:

* Tighten the screws of your computer's cabinet, which act as a grounding mechanism.
* Similarly, tighten the metal cable attachment between the monitor and the computer.
* Try turning off individual components—monitor, modem, and printer, for example—to see if the interference diminishes or goes away. This will help you identify the device emitting RFI.
* Remove completely the cables between various devices. Make sure you disconnect them at both ends. If this helps, you need a better-shielded cable.
* Move the computer farther from the television, or vice versa.

memory. After a character to be displayed is converted in ROM to its display pattern, it is stored in a portion of memory set aside for screen display. This information must remain in memory because to keep a picture on the screen it is necessary for a CRT to constantly "repaint" the images on its screen. It gets the information to do this from the screen memory. If a part of this memory isn't right, you will always see the same problem in the same place on your screen, regardless of what's being displayed.

Both problems are easy to identify and can often be corrected easily by buying a new ROM or RAM chip. ROM chips often mount in a socket, so removal and replacement is a simple task. See the section in Chapter 4 that describes this. RAM chips may also be socketed, but they often are soldered in place. Do-it-yourself removal and replacement of a RAM chip is possible, but unless you feel very comfortable with a solder gun, don't try this operation. You'll have saved plenty of money simply by showing a technician exactly what's wrong. It isn't worth trying desoldering and resoldering if this isn't something with which you are generally comfortable.

Preventing Problems

Do a little experiment: Turn your computer on in a completely dark room, and call up a file or otherwise fill your screen with characters. Now turn the computer off. The image you were displaying will remain on the screen for several seconds, even though the computer is off.

What happens is that the phosphors on the screen, which glow when bombarded with electrons, retain their glow for several seconds. The longer you leave a particular screen display on, the more charged the screen becomes and the longer the image stays on the screen after you turn it off.

This constant bombardment of the screen eventually wears out the phosphors. On some CRTs used day in and day out for exactly the same purpose—airline reservation terminals, for example—you may see an image burned in to the point where you can see it long after the screen is turned off. You, too, can burn an image into your screen and eventually burn your screen out by leaving it on for extended periods when it isn't in use.

To avoid this burnout, turn the screen off when you are not using it. Depending on the type of monitor you have, you may do this by simply turning off the monitor or by adjusting the brightness control until nothing shows on the screen. Some sophisticated computers automatically dim the screen if there is no activity within some prescribed period. As soon as you hit a key, the original display brightness returns.

The low power requirements of LCDs lessen problems associated with heat damage to electrical components, making LCDs remarkably reliable. Because LCDs require a large number of lines to tie each picture element to the display control circuitry, there is a possibility that a line can deteriorate, but this isn't a likely occurrence, because the wiring generally is printed onto a circuit board. If it works after an initial burn-in period, chances are good it will keep going for years.

The only other likely problems are the same as those encountered with a CRT. A bad character-generating ROM chip will result in a bad character being displayed consistently, or at least frequently. Or you may have an area on your screen which is consistently messed up, revealing a problem with the RAM screen memory or the wiring to that particular area.

All in all, an LCD should outlast a CRT by several years, and you should experience far fewer problems with it than with a CRT. With luck, your biggest chore may be to keep the screen sparkling clean.

10
POWER SUPPLIES

A computer's power supply has two basic functions: converting the alternating current (AC) from your wall outlet into the direct current (DC) used by most of the computer's components, and providing electricity in the appropriate form and amounts as required by a computer's various circuits. First, you must understand the difference between AC and DC power. AC shifts from positive to negative polarity once each cycle—it alternates, as the name indicates. (See illustration, page 150.) Standard household current makes this shift sixty times each second. This is known as "60 hertz." (In some areas outside the U.S., 50-hertz electricity is standard.)

TYPICAL POWER SUPPLY COMPONENTS

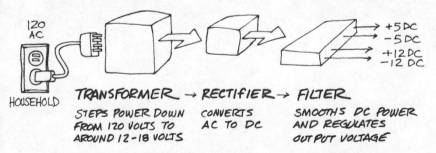

120 AC

HOUSEHOLD

TRANSFORMER → **RECTIFIER** → **FILTER**

STEPS POWER DOWN FROM 120 VOLTS TO AROUND 12-18 VOLTS

CONVERTS AC TO DC

SMOOTHS DC POWER AND REGULATES OUTPUT VOLTAGE

+5 DC
−5 DC
+12 DC
−12 DC

By contrast, DC power is either positive or negative. There is no alternating voltage level or polarity—just a nice, steady flow of electrons. AC power is great for running electric motors, but it isn't very useful in the two-state world of digital electronics, where things are constantly being tested for high or low voltage levels, positive or negative polarity, or simply the presence or absence of a signal or pulse.

The process of converting AC power to DC power isn't very complicated but it requires considerable sophistication because modern digital circuits are quite sensitive to even slight fluctuations in a power supply. It can't be too much or too little, and it should scarcely waver in both quality and quantity. The device used to convert AC power to DC power is a transformer, which takes a pulsating AC current and literally transforms it into a pulsating DC current, which is then filtered to provide a steady DC current.

Power Regulation. Ordinarily, the power you get from your local utility appears to be rather steady and even. You may occasionally notice a flickering of your lights or a dimming of your TV set, but for the most part you probably are unaware of the constant fluctuations in power quality and quantity. Generally, these variations are of little or no consequence to things like toasters, TVs, and turntables.

Things are quite different for a computer. Its central processor, memory, and many other components are quite sensitive to even slight variations in voltage or amperage. Moreover, a loss of power for even a fraction of a second may be too long for the periodic refreshing necessary for the computer to maintain programs and data in memory. Similarly, a power surge can have a disastrous effect on programs and data and literally can burn out sensitive electronic circuits and other components.

Your computer is particularly sensitive to voltage levels. Basic to the operation of digital circuits is the internal testing that occurs constantly, monitoring the computer's signals and comparing them to expected standards. "Was that last signal high or low?" the computer in effect asks itself. "Was it between 3.2 and 5.1 volts (high) or between .02 volts and 1.4 volts (low)? Is it positive or negative? What is the amperage?" This is the heart of electronic digital logic, and, unlike your toaster, it depends upon relatively clean power. As you undertake various tasks—storing something, for example, or sorting something, or simply typing in a few sentences—the computer's power requirements change, too. So the power supply acts something like a combination of a

AC VS. DC VOLTAGE

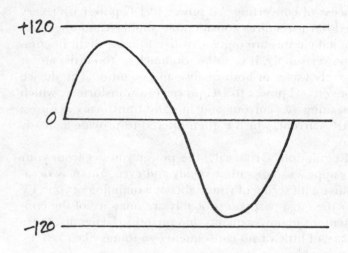

AC VOLTAGE — 1 CYCLE

DC VOLTAGE

traffic cop and a drill sergeant, monitoring the flow of electricity as well as its quality.

To summarize, a power supply:

* converts AC power to DC power;
* protects your system from damage caused by major power surges; and
* ensures a steady supply of power at the right amperage and voltage levels to enable proper functioning of the com-

puter's digital circuits regardless of variations in the supply of power and the machine's constantly varying power needs.

The exact components in a power supply vary considerably from computer to computer. In general, however, they include the incoming AC lines attached to a transformer—a relatively large square or rectangular box. There may be a fuse between the AC plug and the transformer. Between the transformer and the rest of the computer, the power supply looks pretty much like any other circuit board—a handful of free-standing resistors, capacitors, and other discrete components with various integrated-circuit chips thrown in here and there. All of this provides the conversion of AC to DC current and the appropriate filtering and regulating necessary to provide the voltages required by your system.

What Can Go Wrong

A computer's power supply is one of its more vulnerable components. It is subject to considerable stress from the constant variations in the level of power coming to it from the outside world. As the demand for electricity varies in your town throughout the day (there is a much bigger demand during the day, for example, especially in summer), the power company is forced to switch different generators on and off to meet customer requirements.

On a more immediate level, there are local variations that result from your and your neighbors' shifts in electrical demand. When the machine shop down the block switches on its enormous lathes, it will initially draw a lot of current. Perhaps your TV set will flicker slightly as a result. Similarly, if you turn on a hair dryer, toaster, and a few more appliances on the same circuit as your computer, you can achieve the same effect. Both such events result in fairly wide variations in the amount of power delivered to your computer. For very short periods this can be way off the 120 volts we consider as standard.

Environmental conditions also play a major role in the quality of the supply of power. Excessive heat is one major source of stress, for example. Heat is inherent in the process of "stepping the voltage down," as it's called, from 120 volts to the 5- and 12-volt levels used by a computer. Over time, heat tends to weaken components and on a short-term basis can cause electrical circuits to behave in strange ways. While the components in your power supply are generally quite hardy (relative to some of the very sensitive integrated circuits in the rest of your computer), as the system's first line of defense they tend to take a lot more abuse. As with the rest of your machine, dust, smoke, and grime can exacerbate this problem, along with blocked vents, dirty air filters, and operation when the room temperature is too high.

Symptoms of power supply problems can range from the obvious—no power in the system—to very subtle logic errors caused by improper voltage levels. Because it is the starting point for the power in your computer system, upon which everything else depends, as well as a point subject to considerable stress, it is the logical place to begin looking for the cause of almost any problem.

Power Fluctuations. When you aren't getting any power to your system (and have checked obvious things, such as whether or not your household circuit is working and your machine is plugged in), chances are the power supply needs attention. Less dramatic power fluctuations can appear in the form of gradually shrinking images on your CRT. Another clue is change in the sounds made by components with motors, such as a fan, disk drive, or printer. The first question you must answer is whether these symptoms are the result of inadequate power conditioning —a sign of a problem in your power supply—or the result of major power fluctuations, which are beyond your computer's ability to control.

The farther down the line you are from the source of electricity (way out in the boonies, for example) or the closer you are to big industrial users of power (even temporary ones, such as construction sites), the greater your chances of having temporary power supply problems. Similarly, if you live in an area of the country where there are a lot of thunderstorms, you are likely to experience power fluctuations from time to time. Hot summer days will wreak havoc on the power system, as will severe winter storms that bring power lines crashing down.

While a bolt of lightning can wipe out your system—even when it isn't operating—most power supplies are designed to protect your system from the normal ups and downs on the power line. An occasional surge may get through and foul up the logic of a program you are running, causing it to crash or otherwise bomb out on you. Or you might simply lose some data stored in memory to the Great Digital Unknown. Don't panic. Merely seeing your CRT's display shrink every once in a while, or hearing variations in a fan motor, doesn't mean you must take drastic action.

Logic Problems. It's easy to blame the power supply for what appear to be logic problems. Chances are pretty good, however, that operator error and poor programming are more likely causes. Of course, if you experience unexplainable logic foul-ups *and* observe other signs of power fluctuations, such as a shrinking CRT image, the power supply probably is the culprit. But we can't overemphasize that most logic problems stem from operator error and bad programming, not from hardware problems. Unless you see other obvious power supply problems in addition to logic errors, start your diagnosis on the soft side.

Overheating. If your computer gets too hot, then, whether or not this causes observable problems, there may be a difficulty with your power supply. This is all rather relative. Your system may feel hotter on a hot day or in a stuffy room with little air circulation. This is taxing for the system, and anything you can do to get a little air flowing will be helpful. Most computers are designed to minimize heat buildup. For example, heat can be dissipated through well-made designs that spread sources of heat around rather than concentrate them in one place. Vents are used to passively remove heat, while fans actively cool things down.

But if you experience higher-than-usual temperatures or find such things as blocked vents, malfunctioning fans, or merely a buildup of dirt and grime, it could indicate a power supply problem, even though there are no obvious glitches or other malfunctions. An electrical short circuit generates heat, too. The short could be coming from anywhere in the system, not just in the power supply. Besides being a clue to a possible problem, overheating is a serious threat to the health and well-being of your computer—a threat that should not be ignored.

Preventing Problems

Except for disk-cleaning kits, about the only maintenance products advertised in computer magazines are power conditioners, surge protectors, and assorted other power supply protectors and purifiers. Unfortunately, these same publications don't run public service ads for computer cleanliness or warnings from the Society for the Prevention of Cruelty to Computers about the hazards of summer heat to your machine. But there are plenty of opportunities to buy yourself some pricey protection from the misdeeds of your friendly local electric utility.

Are these products worthless? Not quite. Surprisingly, the major cause of computer insurance claims are power blasts that rip through computers, not things like dropped computers or keyboards filled with Coke. Nevertheless, with one exception none of the service engineers we talked to could recall a case where spikes and surges had zapped a computer, although there were several instances where the power supply itself had been annihilated. The collective wisdom of these engineers—with combined experience of several hundred years—was that a normal, working computer's power supply can do everything most low-cost power conditioning and protection devices do, without any added expense.

Moreover, most such devices are overkill: They provide protection against events that wouldn't merely knock out your computer, but probably would blow your building's main circuit breaker right off the wall.

But this may be a bit harsh. If you experience power-related problems that are observable and frequent, not just suspected causes of mysterious occurrences that happen once every blue moon, you probably should get some type of device that provides additional power conditioning. You should, however, put the burden of proof of a product's effectiveness on the dealer or manufacturer. Demand real evidence that what you are buying provides better power regulation than the computer's own power supply. If you are being sold something that gives the same

POWER PROTECTORS

protection and costs more money, you are better off using your hard-earned money to play the ponies.

Protection that effectively eliminates the possibility of power-fluctuation–induced errors is very expensive and unnecessary in most cases, unless you run your machine in an area with incredibly uneven power. For surges, your computer needs about the same amount of protection as you've previously extended to your TV set and stereo. Admittedly, you may have more bucks at stake with your computer. But just think of all the times those horrid spikes and surges have blown your TV to smithereens and expect to lose computers at about the same rate. (OK, your computer's electronics are a bit more sensitive—but not by much.)

Isolating Your Computer. Probably the greatest power supply threat you'll ever face will occur in your own home. When little Johnny (or Janey) plugs the table saw into the same circuit on which you are scrupulously working out your family's financial salvation, don't be surprised if your machine somehow can't find a way for you to retire in a month or two—or even wipes out all the data on your checking accounts you so painstakingly entered.

If possible, try to put your computer on a circuit that won't experience major shifts in electrical load. Ideally, the computer should have a circuit of its very own, but you can get away with simply being careful. Don't crank up the electric popcorn popper until you save your evening's literary masterpiece on disk. A circuit that contains a few lights, a radio, and a clock or two isn't likely to cause problems. Such a circuit is preferable to one with heavy appliances and power tools. Devices with motors are the biggest problems, but toasters, hair dryers, irons, and other appliances with heating elements can do plenty of damage, too.

Keep It Clean. We've said it over and over again, but it's worth repeating: Keep your computer clean. Accumulated dirt and grime cause problems that often look very much like power supply problems. What happens is that as dirt builds up on a computer's components and circuits, it traps heat and things start to go out of whack. Dirt also can cause a circuit to short out by bridging two wires that aren't supposed to touch. With a sufficient dirt buildup, you'll begin experiencing problems that look very much as though you have a flaky power supply or are receiving erratic power.

Weathering the Storm. Depending on where you live, there may be times of the year when you can count on losing power from severe storms. These are times for you to take a break from tinkling your computer's ivories. That doesn't mean not computing during the month of August. To the extent possible, you should shut your machine down when a thunderstorm is imminent and leave it off and *unplugged* until things are back to normal. The same is true when the prevailing winds decide to dump tons of snow intended for the Yukon on your frail city. Use your judgment. You know the kind of weather that knocks out power in your area. When that sort of weather is about to hit, shut your machine down and, in the case of thunderstorms, *unplug your computer from the household AC outlet.* If lightning strikes nearby, it's likely to send a few volts down the power line to your building that, with your luck, will come ripping through anything plugged in. It won't hurt your living room lamp or your toaster a bit, but it could be fatal for your computer.

There always are times when turning your machine off isn't convenient. If you've got to keep going, you've got to keep going. Take a few precautions, however. Be prepared to shut your machine off in a flash if the power gets zapped or if there are noticeable surges. There is a danger that a blast of electricity will come flying down the line and hit your machine when lightning strikes the public power system, but an equally great danger to your computer arises when the power is turned back on after being knocked out. Lightning can send a big surge down the line, but you can get a nearly equal surge when the power company fixes things and flips the switch to "on." It takes a minute or more until things get stabilized. The only guaranteed protection is to turn the computer off and unplug it from the wall.

What You Can and Can't Do

Before you even begin thinking about fixing your power supply, *disconnect the AC power from your machine.* You can feel pretty comfortable checking out your power supply for dirt and grime and removing both with a reversed vacuum cleaner or a can of compressed air. You should also check the circuit board on which the power supply may be mounted for evidence of faulty solder joints, loose solder, scratches, or other damage. Be sure all lines and connectors coming into and out of the power supply are properly connected. But that is about as far as you should go with power supplies. This is serious business: *Don't play around with electricity!*

True, most of the power in your computer is very low DC voltage—about as harmless as a flashlight. You can get away with touching most circuits directly and not get a shock, although you might damage a circuit by causing it to short. This isn't true when you are messing with power supplies, however. There is real live, high-voltage, AC current there that can *kill.* In most cases, you'll find your power supply sealed away with warning labels admonishing you not to unseal it. This is good advice. If you are an electronics whiz *and* have the appropriate technical manuals to steer you through things, you might be able to usefully poke around a power supply and find a bad IC, capacitor, burned-out component, or a loose wire or connection. But if you are not at this level of competence, simply stay away from inside the unit.

Without the appropriate technical manuals, there generally isn't a lot you can do to test a power supply. Troubleshooting comes down to identifying symptoms of a bad power supply.

Occasionally, you'll find lines coming off the power supply marked at certain voltage levels—typically 5 volts and 12 volts. You can check these with a voltmeter to see if they are correct. But remember: If the incoming voltage is way out of line, you might end up with readings that are off but still have a good power supply.

You probably are limited to two repairs: total replacement of the power supply or replacement of a fuse between the AC line and the transformer. But don't replace a fuse until you have found out what caused it to blow and have corrected the problem. And before you go to the expense of replacing a power supply— they can cost upward of $100, not including installation—try testing the computer at some other location, just to assure yourself there is something wrong with the computer, not with the external power being supplied your machine.

Your power supply's fuse is either inside the power supply box, where it's inaccessible, or outside, where it's accessible. Replacing a fuse is simple and straightforward but requires that you use an exact duplicate of the one that burned out. If you have a 5-amp fuse, for example, you must replace it with another 5-amp fuse— not a 10-amp or a 1-amp. If it is a fast-burn fuse, it has to be replaced with another fast-burn fuse.

A fuse may blow because the incoming power is excessive, but more typically because of some problem that draws excessive power from the AC line. Sometimes this is just a fluke, and you can safely replace the fuse without further action. Always check to see if something is causing a short circuit or if an IC has blown. If you don't, you will probably just blow the fuse again. You might even damage something.

Here are some possible causes of power supply problems:

* If you are not getting any power to your system and you are sure the AC outlet is working, you can be sure there is something wrong with your power supply.
* If you are experiencing intermittent logic errors—programs going astray or the system doing other screwy things—exhaust all other possibilities before settling on the power supply as the source of the problem. While symptomatic of power supply problems, logic errors also are symptoms of

On and Off Again

There is a debate among computer-types about whether you should leave your computer on at all times or turn it off when you're not using it.

In the old days of computing, when machines were behemoth beasts, you never turned the power off. It took too much power to bring such systems back up, and you risked surging other electronic equipment when you turned it on or off. But back then computers cost millions, and you simply didn't want to risk damage.

It still is true that turning equipment on and off strains it, but not that much. On the other hand, many computers today rely on passive heat dissipation—they have no fans and are subject to overheating problems. Leaving it on causes strain, too, by maintaining the level of heat. The net effect is that it is a good idea to leave your machine on when you expect to get back to it in an hour or so but to turn it off if you plan to be away for longer periods. Watch out for heat. If heat tends to be a problem, by all means turn the computer off when you aren't using it.

If you are in an area with an erratic power supply or periods of bad weather when power outages are likely, be sure not only to turn your machine off, but to disconnect it from the AC power outlet.

many other digital diseases. Check out these other possibilities before you shell out money for a new power supply.

* If you suspect the problem lies in the AC power and are swayed by all the advertising aimed at selling power-conditioning devices, make the salesperson document the additional power conditioning of a device compared directly with your machine's own ratings. You are interested in the range of voltage against which the device provides protection and the speed at which it responds to a surge. Both figures are relative, however, depending on the range of protection offered by your computer's power supply. It doesn't matter,

for example, if Power Protecto X is ten times faster and better than Power Protecto Y if both duplicate the protection already afforded your machine by its internal power-regulating devices.

Actual replacement of a power supply is usually pretty straightforward, although there can be a twist or two that may put it outside the realm of things in which you wish to involve yourself. Generally, the unit is simply bolted in place, with the incoming power cord connected to the power supply with a couple screws. At the other end, the power supply connects to the computer with a cable connector or a couple screws.

Always disconnect the unit from the AC power before attempting to remove or install the power supply. Always.

If your power supply is connected in some other way—directly soldered, for example—consider having it replaced professionally. Should you fail to properly solder a connection, you may seriously damage the power supply, to say nothing of the entire system. As long as you are pretty certain it is the power supply that is the problem, you should feel more than comfortable taking your machine to a competent shop for replacement.

11
PRINTERS

There are many kinds of printers, but they all do basically the same thing: transfer information from your computer to a piece of paper. If it's so easy, then, why are there so many different kinds of printers, and why are they all so complicated?

In reality, printing is a bit more complex than merely transferring information. The process goes something like this: First, the computer transmits a signal indicating it has a character it wants printed. If the printer tells the computer it is ready to accept the character, the character is transferred from an area in random-access memory to a serial or parallel port, down a cable, and into another interface on the printer. From there, the printer—usually using its own little computer—transfers a pattern for the character to a print head, which strikes an inked ribbon or transfers the image directly to paper. Then the print head advances itself one character to the right or down the page one or more lines.

One major classification of printers divides them into impact and nonimpact printers. Either the print head strikes a ribbon, which transfers an image to paper (impact), or the image is transferred thermally or by squirting ink on paper (nonimpact) or, more recently, by charging the paper with a pattern that then attracts a toner material which is heated so it remains where you want it—the same principal behind many copy machines.

Each of these methods requires that a character first be sent from the computer. The printer then prints the character itself (in the case of daisy wheel and thimble letter-quality printers) or figures out (in the case of ink-jet, dot-matrix, and laser printers) what pattern must be generated to actually produce the character. Along with characters, the printer also receives various instructions to move over a few spaces or down a few lines, execute a carriage return, or eject a finished page.

Using an on-board computer—a microprocessor, some memory, and some interface circuitry—the printer keeps track of where it is, instructs its motors to move the print head to a particular position, and then instructs various electromagnetic solenoids (switches) to activate themselves to cause the character to be banged against a ribbon and the paper. Signals are sent to another motor to move the paper up or down.

What you have, then, is a couple of motors for horizontal and vertical print head positioning (and one to spin a daisy wheel or thimble), a computer to control all of this, and a slew of detectors that determine if your ribbon is working, if there is paper in the printer, and (sometimes) if the print head made it back to the left margin when the printer executed a carriage return.

The print head usually rides on a metal rod and is pushed or pulled along by some kind of belt. Typically this uses an independent power supply, rather than drawing on the computer for electricity.

What Can Go Wrong

A printer is, in many ways, the most vulnerable component in any computer system. First, it has a lot of moving parts. Impact printers do a lot of moving and banging. Wear and tear are inevitable and misalignment certain after a few months' use. Many parts are throw-away. You bang the print head to death, for example, then buy another. The various motors wear themselves out and must be replaced. Ditto with the machine's belts.

On top of all this, you have virtually the same problems as with a computer because the printer itself is likely to have a computer. Finally, you have the problem of getting the printer to communicate properly with your computer—no mean feat, in many cases. The entire operation takes place in a very difficult environment, filled with paper dust particles and vibrations.

The above notwithstanding, most printers on the market are incredibly reliable, especially when you consider the relative hostility of their environments. Many experience a remarkable eight thousand hours—the equivalent of a full year of around-the-clock use—before they break down, and even then they take only minutes to fix. With a printer maintenance manual and the right tools, almost anyone can fix a printer and do so in a matter of minutes.

Because of the vast number of printers available for microcomputers, we can go only so far in describing the particulars of printers; each manufacturer, it seems, has taken a slightly different approach to how it puts things together. On the whole, printer manufacturers' maintenance manuals tend to be relatively readable, and, if your printer's central processor hasn't gone down, you often can use a series of built-in diagnostic tests that help nail down problems. Many manufacturers make their parts available to printer owners. (You usually can find the manufacturer's address in the user manual provided with the machine.)

Repairs are typically simple. Most involve pulling a modular component out of the printer and replacing it with a new one. This can be a bit expensive, but it will cost considerably more if you have a technician do it for you, and chances are the technician won't even try to repair the part, even if that would be cheaper than replacing it. Because parts tend to be readily available—unlike most components of your computer—there's basically no reason not to give it a shot.

Getting Started

Getting your printer up and running will probably be the most frustrating part of its operation. Printer manufacturers are forced to provide a wide range of options for their machines because they'll be hooked up to any of a number of different computers. If you buy your printer at a retail store, insist that the store set everything up for you—and make them demonstrate, if possible, that computer and printer are working correctly, preferably using your software.

If you buy mail order, you're on your own. Be prepared for a few hassles. Unless you've mastered cables and interfaces (see Chapter 6), you should buy a ready-made cable specifically packaged for your printer and computer rather than a general-purpose cable. You'll pay a little more for this, but if you place any value on your time, rest assured you'll come out ahead.

Your printer's user's manual likely contains detailed information on how to set the switches necessary to make a printer and computer compatible. For the most part, these switches take care of the basics: the number of bits (seven or eight) your computer will be sending with each character; whether or not it will send a line feed with a carriage return; special character sets (English, French, etc.); and on and on.

Most settings can be changed by sending a predetermined group of codes to the printer from the computer keyboard. You needn't worry about this, however, because the individual applications software (word processing, spreadsheets, etc.) should take care of this when you first set up the program.

Devil Dust

Under normal use, a printer's motor and print head can wear out, belts become worn, and everything gets out of alignment. You must either replace them yourself or have a professional do it for you. You can extend the lives of these components by making some adjustments if you've invested in the printer's maintenance manual. You also can keep things humming if you religiously clean your printer.

Dust doesn't affect belts directly—they'll stretch regardless of how clean the machine. But almost every other component, including the control and interface circuit boards, can be affected by paper dust. The effect is devilish.

If you regularly vacuum and blow dust from the printer, you may double the time between failures, although you'll probably still have to replace the print head in an impact printer from time to time in spite of your efforts at cleanliness. The printer is one place where $4.00 cans of air can save a lot of dough. Simply send a concentrated blast to get the paper dust out of the print head mechanism; you'll find this a bit difficult with a vacuum cleaner running in reverse.

PREVENTIVE MAINTENANCE FOR PRINTERS

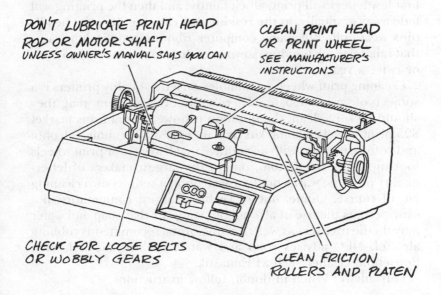

DON'T LUBRICATE PRINT HEAD
ROD OR MOTOR SHAFT
UNLESS OWNER'S MANUAL SAYS YOU CAN

CLEAN PRINT HEAD
OR PRINT WHEEL
SEE MANUFACTURER'S
INSTRUCTIONS

CHECK FOR LOOSE BELTS
OR WOBBLY GEARS

CLEAN FRICTION
ROLLERS AND PLATEN

Head Cleaners

There are several commercial products on the market for cleaning print heads, particularly the daisy wheel- and thimble-type heads. Isopropyl alcohol may be just as good, but be careful. If the manufacturer says "you must use my product," feel free to check around for something else that may be cheaper. But if the manufacturer says *never* use such and such cleaner on the head, believe it. The reason is that print head manufacturers use many different types of plastic and metal. Some materials react chemically with certain cleaners, and you'll be left with a ruined print head.

In most cases alcohol will do the trick, but make sure the manufacturer has not specifically warned against it. If there is no prohibition against its use, you are probably safe. You may use alcohol to clean the platen, too. (The platen is the black rubber round thing that turns as you move the paper up and down.)

You can clean a dot-matrix print head by removing the ribbon, inserting a piece of paper, and then "printing" a few lines. The first few letters will print, albeit faintly, and then the printing will fade away gradually, as the residue that can clog the print head's pins wears off. But many computer ribbons contain lubricants that minimize ink buildup, so you needn't do this more than once or twice a year.

Cleaning print wheels or thimbles on letter-quality printers is a subject of great debate. There's no disagreement that they should be kept clean; the question is how. Several firms market $25 print-wheel cleaning kits that are essentially rubbing alcohol and cotton, perhaps with an additive that leaves your print wheels looking shiny. But Diablo, one of the largest makers of letter-quality printers, warns not to use alcohol; it sells its own cleaning kit, of course. Qume, one of Diablo's largest competitors, not only permits the use of alcohol but suggests that soap and water may do the trick just as well. Smith-Corona recommends rubbing alcohol. NEC advises soap and water, rubbing alcohol, or a household cleaner such as Fantastik.

Our advice: When in doubt, follow instructions.

Lubricants

The rod on which the print head travels looks like a good place to put a lubricant. So do the shafts of the various motors on a printer. *Don't lubricate either place* unless this is specifically called for by the manufacturer. If it is, follow its instructions explicitly as to the type and amount of lubricant. In fact, to be safe, use a bit less than it specifies.

Before doing any lubrication, clean the old lubricant off with some alcohol. Then apply as little lubricant as you can. Overlubing merely creates a nice gooey place for paper dust to build up.

Spotting Problems

After extended use of your printer, you are likely to run into problems. With average failure time running up in the one-year range (based on twenty-four-hour-a-day use), you may be lucky enough to go for several years without problems.

Keeping your machine clean will extend this time. You should also consider bringing your printer in for a tune-up, even when you aren't experiencing specific problems, or do it yourself with a printer maintenance manual. What you or the repair facility will be doing is checking for wear and adjusting the belt tension and motor action as well as replacing any worn parts. With all the banging around a printer does, you should also check for loose nuts and screws as well as reseat any socketed ICs.

Everyone has paper-feeding problems with printers. If the paper-feeding mechanism works at all, you must find the correct paper positioning and make sure the paper feeds in a straight line. There is no magic here; just carefully line up the paper—and try to keep it there.

Shady Characters

You'll also run into problems with ribbons. They, of course, wear out. They also occasionally jam, and you'll find it easier to throw them out than to try to free the ribbon. If proper ribbon tension isn't maintained, you'll get shadows and smeared characters. Most such problems are illustrated in the user's manual, but even without it you probably can figure out how to correct things just by close examination. If your ribbon is too tight, it may prevent the head from banging against the paper, with the result that you get a very faint image. A loose ribbon, on the other hand, causes shadows and smears.

Sometimes you may lose a character during communications between the computer and the printer. When this happens you are, in fact, more than likely to drop several characters at a crack. Unless your cables are loose, this is probably just an electrical fluke and nothing to lose sleep over. If it happens often, you may need professional service.

If the printer drops a lot of characters or prints assorted garbage, suspect the cables if you are sure the software you're using has worked before with the printer. If it is new software, try another program that you know works.

Throughout the troubleshooting process, you almost always have the option of running the printer, independent of the computer, through some sort of self-test series. Doing this may help establish where the problem lies.

Look for patterns. Is a particular character messed up all the time? Is there a certain frequency to the problem—every thirty-six characters, for example? The first case may indicate a bad character memory chip; the second could result from a bad spot in the printer's buffer memory.

In either case, cleaning is a good first step. Then reseat any socketed chips—especially character-set ROM chips. They are likely to be of the plug-in variety.

The problem could be more subtle—a flaky control program or a bad control circuit line, for example. You can use the same techniques outlined in Chapter 4, on the central processor, to try to pin this down, or you may be lucky enough to have a printer self-test routine that can identify this kind of problem.

And don't overlook the possibility that your print wheel (on a letter-quality printer) or print head (on a dot-matrix printer) may be dirty.

Moving Around

The next most frequent printer problem involves the movement of paper and print head, including the print head's return to the left-margin position.

The first thing to look for here is any obvious mechanical problem—a loose belt, a slipping gear, and the like. Difficulty with either horizontal or vertical positioning can be the result of a problem in the printer control program or the printer's control circuit. But this isn't as likely to be the source of a problem as something being loose, stretched, or worn.

The motors that help position the print head can wear out. When this happens, chances are the incorrect positioning will tend to be off uniformly—all characters overlapping each other, for example. If the pattern isn't uniform, check to see if a belt is loose.

The friction roller is another source of problems. If you're not using a tractor feed, you can run into the same sort of problems with a friction roller as you do with an ordinary typewriter. A combination of vibrations and dust can create a roller so slippery that the paper will slide through and not advance properly. You can clean the roller with alcohol or acetone (nail polish remover) in most cases, but check the user's manual to be sure that these won't ruin the roller.

The platen is run by a motor that locks it into place so printing will appear in a straight line, then advances the platen precisely when it's time to move down (or up) a line. Don't overpower the motor by turning it when the printer is on. If you have to turn the platen extensively, turn the motor off first. You'll put a little more wear and tear on the on/off switch, but that's one of the cheapest things to replace if it wears out.

Watch the print head carefully. You'll see that when it moves, it does so in tiny increments controlled by a stepper motor. When the head returns to the left margin, however, it tends to fly back instead of stepping, relying on some sort of left-margin guide or sensor to correctly position itself. If you routinely have left-margin problems, the home sensor may be out of whack. There are a number of ways printers sense the left margin, ranging from a photocell–light-emitting diode combination to various barriers or belt clamps that can break or come loose. Generally, however, intermittent left-margin problems are like characters gone astray —they come with the territory and are generally not cause for concern.

Cables between computer devices can act as antennas that pick up radio frequencies, disrupting the operation of the equipment. (See We Interrupt This Program . . . on page 144.) Printer cables can be particularly troublesome, especially if they extend longer than 10 feet. If you live in suburban or rural areas, however, where radio interference isn't much of a problem, you can extend them to as long as 20 feet without problem.

In the end, printer maintenance really comes down to keeping it clean. After considerable use, you'll likely have to replace the print head and a belt or two, but that should be about it. If you keep it spotlessly clean, most other problems may never occur. Get out that vacuum right now, and try to be religious about using it frequently. There is no danger in overcleaning your printer.

PART III

RESOURCES

12
HOW TO FIND
A GOOD REPAIR SHOP

Getting professional repairs can be a forbidding experience. And an expensive one, if you don't watch out.

If you've ever brought a car to a mechanic, you know the frustration of getting repairs for a complex machine you don't really understand. It's bad enough you don't really know what's wrong with it. What's worse is that you're at the mercy of someone who can't explain your machine's problem in terms you can comprehend. With great trepidation, you must leave your equipment with a stranger, not knowing what's wrong, whether or not this person is capable of solving the problem, how many times you'll have to bring it back before the problem is fixed, and how much the whole experience will cost.

Let's face it: There's a lot you can't do to fix your computer. And there's a lot you *shouldn't* do. After all, we're talking about an incredibly high piece of tech, one with few moving parts; most of what gets done is accomplished by electrons traveling through circuits at breakneck speed. While it may look rather staid inside your machine, there's an awful lot going on that you can inadvertently—and irreparably—disrupt if you don't know what you're doing. Sometimes it's best to let the pros take over.

But just who and where are these "pros"? While computer repair shops are popping up like mushrooms after a rainstorm, there's a good chance none has yet opened in your neighborhood, perhaps not even in your city. The manufacturer of your equipment may be located half a continent away or overseas. The place where you purchased your equipment may not provide service. (Some stores that claim to provide service actually pack up your equipment and ship it off to a regional service facility.)

Even if your dealer does make repairs, it's often hard to know just what you're getting into. Is the dealer authorized to make repairs on your make and model? Be careful: Some "authorized" dealers are really authorized only to pack up your equipment and send it off to the aforementioned service facility. (By the way, understand that being "authorized" and being "competent" are two very different things.)

What if you can't give up your equipment for more than a day or two? You certainly won't want to ship it to some faraway facility. Even if it's repaired locally in a matter of days, you may need a loaner while your equipment is on the mend. And what about hourly rates, guarantees for work performed, and on-site services that come to you?

The good news is that competent, affordable repair can be found.

Before You Panic

The search takes a bit of work, but the small investment in time will be more than paid back in reliable, affordable repairs. But before you begin, you must ask four basic questions.

* *Is this trip necessary?* Your equipment's "problem" may be the result of a number of problems from a number of sources, ranging from not being plugged in to not being operated properly. As stated previously, an apparent malfunction with a piece of hardware may actually be the result of a software problem. Before you go through the effort of bringing your computer or related equipment in for repairs, you should exhaust two other principal resources: the manuals for both hardware and software, and your own intuition. Go back and read Chapter 1, What's Wrong with My Computer?

* *What's your diagnosis?* You'll save a great deal of time and money by coming up with one or more likely diagnoses of your computer's problem. The more specific the diagnosis, the better. Among the information that will help a technician make repairs are specific details of the problem. For example: Does the problem occur only after the computer has

been on for a while, or is it consistent? Does the monitor display an error message when the problem occurs? Have you recently made any changes in your computer system, either in software or hardware? Was the computer recently moved or dropped or did it suffer any other type of unusual event? Such specific information can help a technician zero in on what may seem like an insoluble mystery. But if you don't know, don't fake it. Your attempt to sound knowledgeable could send a technician on an expensive (for you) wildgoose chase.

* *Is help just a phone call away?* You'd be surprised how often it is. Many hardware and software manufacturers maintain technical service experts who can help solve problems via telephone. So do a growing number of computer stores. If you have diagnosed your problem to the point that you can describe it as specifically as possible, you may be able to get a fix on the phone. If you do find someone who is helpful, be sure to get his or her name so you can get additional information as needed. (Jot the name and number down in your Maintenance Log.) By the way, many companies have unadvertised toll-free "800" numbers that may not even appear in their documentation or owner's manuals. Check with "800" information (800-555-1212) to see if such a number exists.

* *Have you exhausted sources of free help?* Don't forget about users' groups and their electronic bulletin boards. Despite all the media hype about such bulletin boards becoming trading places for stolen telephone credit card numbers and the like, a lot of what actually transpires on such boards involves the exchange of troubleshooting information about specific hardware and software products. If you float your problem out among your fellow computer users, you may find not only that you're not alone in your misery, but that some dedicated hacker spent the better part of three sleepless nights solving the problem—and is willing to pass along his solution so that you don't have to do the same thing.

Six Things Your Repairperson Would Like to Tell You

* **Read the manual.** Granted, most are written by semiliterate-types who probably should be relegated to writing the federal tax code, but you may find some golden nuggets of information that can save your technician's time— and your money. As we've said repeatedly, a large number of computer problems result from not following instructions.

* **Be specific.** The more accurately you can describe a problem, the easier it will be to fix. Don't come in and announce, "My printer's broken." The biggest problem is with intermittent problems—those that come and go without explanation. Try to determine a pattern: Do they happen after the computer's been on a long time? Do they

Making the Search

There are several places to look for a good shop. First and foremost, you should find the location of the nearest authorized service center for your equipment. You can get names of authorized shops from the manufacturer of your computer (the names may appear in your owner's manual). Be sure, however, that service will be done "on-site" as opposed to being shipped out to a central repair facility. But don't stop your search there, even if there's an authorized shop around the block. You should get at least two or three possibilities before making your choice.

There are other places to look, each of which can be a good choice.

happen after you perform some type of operation, such as printing a document or retrieving a file? It is with such information that technicians fix things quickly and effectively.

* **Move it gently.** When you bring your equipment in for repairs, put it in a box and secure it so it won't rattle around. Bumping and jarring the computer as you carry it around unprotected can cause additional problems.

* **Fixing computers is as much art as science.** If you've read through this book, that fact should be crystal clear; yet computer owners still expect things to be fixed perfectly the first time. Don't expect too much too quickly. It may be unfair to expect a technician to resolve in an hour what resulted from years of abuse and neglect.

* **No technician does everything right all the time.** There are less-than-scrupulous technicians, of course, but the complexities of computers are immense. The best technicians aren't those who never make mistakes, but those who make sure no customer is dissatisfied.

* **There's no correlation between price and quality.** This has been documented in study after study.

* Your *computer dealer* may have a shop or may be affiliated with one. A shop affiliated with a dealer may be a good choice because there will be *two* organizations accountable for the service—the dealer and the repair shop. Some shops give priority to work sent by a dealer.

* An *independent repair shop* may be a good choice if it specializes in servicing your type of equipment or your type of repair. Some shops may deal with only a few models, while others may specialize in specific types of repairs, such as on disk drives or on printers.

* *Independent or moonlighting technicians* may be a good choice for simple problems, such as aligning a disk drive or adjusting a printer. One source for such individuals is a local users' group specializing in your type of equipment. Often, users' groups have arrangements with technicians who perform service for members' machines at a special rate.

In general, it's best to use shops that come recommended from friends or dealers. When you contact a recommended shop, make it known that you came to it through a reference.

Getting Good Service

Once you've chosen a shop, there are a few more things you can do to increase your chances of getting the best service.

* *Call ahead.* As with doctors and car mechanics, you may get better service if you call ahead and make an appointment.
* *Get everything in writing.* That includes estimates, of course, but it also includes details about what work was done, what parts were installed (including serial numbers, if appropriate), and what warranties apply to parts and labor. Warranties for new replacement parts should be as long as those for the original parts—typically ninety days; rebuilt parts may have shorter warranties.
* *Pay by credit card.* If you use plastic and later discover that the repairs weren't done to your satisfaction, you'll have some leverage to get the problem corrected. Under federal credit laws, you have the right not to pay disputed bills. You must follow specific rules, however, which are outlined periodically on your credit card bills.
* *Pass the word.* If you do find competent, affordable service, tell your friends, and let the shop know you are doing so. You'll be richly rewarded in gratitude from your fellow computer users, most of whom probably are frustrated in their searches for good service. Tell your friends to use your name as a reference when they call for service. That way you'll also score Brownie points with your technician, assuring good service the next time you need a fix.

13

WARRANTIES, INSURANCE, AND SERVICE CONTRACTS

If you've ever bought a new or used car, you know the troubles warranties can bring. One big problem, for example, is that not everything that doesn't work right is "under warranty," even if the warranty period is far from expired. A particular component —a disk drive, for example—may simply stop working during the warranty period, something you believe is fully covered by the manufacturer. As the warranty instructs, you bring it to an authorized service shop for free warranty repairs.

But no: The disk drive's problem, according to the shop, is that it came within fifty yards of a peanut butter and jelly sandwich— an event strictly forbidden under the warranty's terms, thus voiding the warranty. You, not the manufacturer, must foot the repair bill.

While it's true that a sandwich probably won't void a warranty (any more than its mere proximity to a disk drive would put the drive out of whack), there are things of which you must be careful, lest you risk the wrath of manufacturers when it comes time for warranty repairs. Example: A warranty for one of the leading computer manufacturers states, "The warranty is void if the Equipment's case or cabinet has been opened, or if the Equipment . . . has been subjected to improper or abnormal use."

While you might question the manufacturer's real intention in forbidding you from even *opening* the cabinet—it's probably based more on its desire to corner the market on its machines' repairs than on its fears that you might hurt something—the message is implicit, if not explicit: While under warranty, a computer or related product is under strict conditions which, if violated, could mean that the repair bill must be paid by you, not it.

Before you bring your computer in for warranty repairs, you might save yourself a lot of trouble by reading the warranty first.

Warranty Types

It's important to know that there are three basic types of warranties, not all of which need even be in writing.

Written warranties come with most computer products, although they aren't legally required. As indicated above, the protection offered by written warranties varies greatly and is subject to a wide range of conditions. Here are some questions to keep in mind when examining a warranty.

* What parts and repair problems are covered? (Sometimes there are strict limitations to the problems covered under warranty.)
* Are any expenses excluded from coverage? (Some warranties require that you pay labor or shipping costs.)
* How long does the warranty last? (The periods are usually different for parts and labor.)
* What must you do to get service? (Some companies require that you ship the defective machine off to some faraway place; others offer neighborhood service.)
* What will the company do if the product fails? (It might repair it, replace it, or simply return your money.)
* Does the warranty cover consequential damages? (Most don't. If a disk drive failure made you miss your income tax filing deadline, the product manufacturer won't be liable for penalties and interest levied by the IRS.)
* Are there any other conditions or limitations? (These can vary widely.)

Spoken warranties are those that come from a salesperson—that the store will provide free repairs for any problem during the first ninety days, for example. If this claim is not in writing, however, you may not be able to get the promise fulfilled. You should have the salesperson put any such claims in writing, even if only a brief notation on your estimate, receipt, or bill of sale. Or write it down yourself and have the salesperson sign or initial it. Otherwise, don't count on the promise actually being kept.

Implied warranties are required by state law, and all states have them. Almost every purchase you make is covered by an implied warranty. The most common type is called a "warranty of merchantability." This means that if the seller promises that the product you bought does something, it should really do that. A computer should compute; a printer should print. Another type of implied warranty is called a "warranty of fitness for a particular purpose." If you purchase a printer, for example, with the understanding that it will work with your type of computer, that is an implied warranty.

Another type of implied warranty is an expressed warranty. It's common, for example, for a salesperson to demonstrate a piece of software on a machine with more memory than the one you actually use. If this isn't disclosed and you buy the software, you may be entitled under federal law to a refund, along with damages resulting from having relied on the recommendation, as well as the difference between the cost of an adequate system and the one that was recommended. You'll probably have to go to court to receive all such compensation, of course, but this is what the law says you're entitled to. At the very least, you should get your money back.

Even if something doesn't come with a written warranty, it still is covered by an implied warranty unless the product is marked "as is" or the seller otherwise indicates in writing that no warranty is given. Several states, including Kansas, Maine, Maryland, Massachusetts, Vermont, and West Virginia, and the District of Columbia do not permit "as is" sales.

Implied warranty coverage can last as long as four years, although the length of coverage varies from state to state. In seven states—Kansas, Maine, Maryland, Massachusetts, Mississippi, Vermont, and West Virginia—implied warranties may not be limited to the duration of the written warranty, if the duration is shorter than the periods allowed by those states. A lawyer or a state consumer protection office can provide more information about implied warranty coverage in your state.

A summary of product warranties for selected computers, printers, and modems can be found starting on page 185.

We have yet to discuss warranties for software, which usually contain so many qualifications and disclaimers they are virtually worthless. Typical language states: "This program is provided as is, without warranty of any kind, either expressed or implied, including, but not limited to, the implied warranty of merchantability and fitness for any particular purpose." In other words, "You paid for it, it's yours." Can you imagine purchasing a computer or any other product that contained such a "warranty"?

A Matter of Policy

You may never consider insuring your computer, but, when you think about it, it makes good sense. For one thing, unless the sum total of your personal computing activities consists of defending Earth from alien invaders of the universe, you've probably amassed a small treasure trove of software, the total value of which may be hundreds, perhaps thousands, of dollars. What would happen, for example, if your dog accidently decided it needed nourishment in the form of a small black square of plastic (or whatever floppy disks are encased in)? Where would you be if a gin and tonic accidently spilled all over your bridge club mailing list?

You'd be out a lot of money, or time, or both.

Even barring such calamities, it's important to remember that your computer and related equipment comprise a rather pricey lot—costlier, perhaps, than your TV, stereo, or even your car. And more fragile than any of them. For such reasons, you may need to have it covered against the inevitable bumps, drops, spills, and assorted other things that cause otherwise healthy computers to get sick or even to die.

A good homeowner's (or renter's) policy will cover your computer equipment, although not necessarily for business use of a computer kept at home. Many major insurance companies, including Aetna, Kemper, Nationwide, Prudential, and State Farm, automatically include computers in homeowner's policies; if yours does not, you can add a rider for a nominal fee, typically

$35 or so annually. However, there may be some exclusions. For example, a regular homeowner's policy won't cover data loss or equipment damage resulting from a power surge. Nor will it cover household accidents, such as a dog-chewed floppy disk or a keyboard bathed in Sprite. Nor will it, probably, cover the cost of losing software that you've written yourself; commercial software usually is covered, however.

But if you're using your computer for business purposes, homeowner's policies may be of no help. (Actually, some homeowner's policies will insure your system for the percent you use your computer for *personal* use, the opposite of how the Internal Revenue Service lets you deduct your home computer for *business* use. In other words, if you take a tax deduction for business use of a home computer, your homeowner's policy may not totally cover your computer.) A number of insurance companies have created policies specially suited for business computer users, whether used at home or the office.

Be careful, however: Many business insurance policies covering computers are overpriced. It's not uncommon to pay $150 or more annually for a business computer policy, while you can get identical coverage for much less. In this case, it really pays to shop around. One company worth checking out is Safeware (P.O. Box 02211, Columbus, OH 43202; 800-848-3469). Safeware's policy, underwritten by Fireman's Fund, reimburses insured computer owners for the full replacement cost of the equipment or software at the time of the loss. The cost: $60 for up to $5,000 of coverage, with $15 for each $3,000 of additional coverage.

Make sure that a specialized policy meets your needs. Among the things to consider:

* If you're using your computer for business, you may want to insure not only the hardware and software, but the data that you've spent hours inputting (or paid someone else to input). Not all policies (including Safeware's) cover this kind of loss. One that does is offered by Sentry Insurance (1800 North Point Drive, Stevens Point, WI 54481; 715-346-6617), which pays up to $1,000 for data stored that is lost or destroyed due to a covered loss.

* Some policies pay for the cost of renting equipment while yours is being fixed or replaced.
* If you have a portable computer, make sure it's covered when it's being transported. If you transport it in your car, check your car insurance policy to see if the computer is covered against theft and accidents.
* If you're moving your home or office, it's worth making sure your computer equipment is covered during the move, a time when computers can easily get jarred, bumped, or otherwise mishandled.

Buying Time

Another type of insurance policy is known as an extended warranty or maintenance contract. While such devices won't reimburse you for accidents or mishandling, they will cover repairs and maintenance for things that go wrong after the warranty has expired.

There's a good case to be made that such insurance doesn't make sense for most home computer owners. A typical extended service policy costs 10 to 12 percent of the retail cost of the equipment being covered per year. If your computer, printer, and modem cost $3,000, then you'd pay $300 to $360 under a typical plan to have them covered. That's a lot of money when you consider that you could go for a year or two without any repairs. Even if you did have a major problem that took four hours to fix at $60 an hour, you'd still come out ahead. There are some bargains, however. AppleCare, the extended service program offered by Apple Computer, offers parts, labor, and unlimited repairs for about $50 a year for models like the Apple IIe, IIc, and Macintosh. Moreover, the policies are renewable for as long as you'd like.

If you own two or more computers, you may well benefit from one of the growing number of independent service companies that are sprouting up faster than you can say "microprocessor." Detecting big profit potential, corporate giants like Xerox, TRW, Western Union, RCA, Control Data, General Electric, and MAI/Sorbus are getting into the so-called third-party repair business.

Joining them are a host of start-up franchise firms, with names like Computer Doctor, Computer Repair Corporation, and Serviceland. Most of these organizations offer a wide range of service contracts. Costs vary widely, too, depending on such things as the type of equipment, how far you are from the service center, how quickly the company guarantees it will respond to your call, and whether loaners are available while your equipment is being mended. Most companies offer different rates for "carry-in" service (where you bring your equipment to them) and "on-site" service (where they do repairs at your home or office). Some companies also have "mail-in" service. At least one company offers a combination: "courier" service, in which it picks up and delivers your equipment but does repairs in its own shop.

Because most companies are relatively new at the repair business and because of the growing demand for repair services, the quality of service available under service contracts varies as widely as prices, although there isn't necessarily a correlation between price and quality. A report by Service Research Group in 1984 identified 132 service companies. The products most often covered for service were Apple computers and IBM-PCs, along with various printers, terminals, and word processors. The average response time to a service request was about seventeen hours, although the response time ranged from one to sixty hours. The average per-hour charge was $53.68, with about one hour as the average minimum charge.

The market is confusing even for those in the business. An executive at one large computer manufacturer, quoted in *Business Computing* magazine, put it this way: "Trying to figure out how to service personal computers sold through distributors is like trying to figure out how to get out of Vietnam."

Product Manufacturers

Here is a list of major computer and computer product manufacturers, including their addresses and information about their warranties, extended service policies, service, and the availability of technical manuals. This information is subject to change, so it's important to check with these companies for up-to-date information.

COMPUTERS

Apple Computer, 20525 Mariani Ave., Cupertino, CA 95014.
Warranty: 90 days parts and labor.
Extended Service Policy: Apple offers AppleCare carry-in service after warranty has expired. AppleCare is available through dealers, with the price fixed by Apple. AppleCare may be purchased for the entire unit or for individual components. The policy is renewable and includes parts, labor, and unlimited repairs.
Service: Available from dealers and Apple's regional facilities. Call 800-538-9696 for locations.
Technical Manuals: None.

Columbia Data Products, 9150 Rumsey Road, Columbia, MD 21045.
Warranty: 90 days parts and labor.
Extended Service Policy: None.
Service: Some dealers are authorized to service, as are Bell & Howell depots. Call 800-638-7866 for locations.

Commodore Business Machines, 1200 Wilson Drive, West Chester, PA 19380.
Warranty: 90 days parts and labor.
Extended Service Policy: None offered through Commodore, but individual dealers may have their own service plans available.
Service: Available by mail through Commodore or through authorized shops. Call 215-436-4200 for locations and troubleshooting. Some mass-market retailers, such as K mart and Sears, exchange new equipment for inoperable equipment.

Compaq, 20333 FM 149, Houston, TX 77070.
Warranty: 90 days parts and labor.
Extended Service Policy: Available for 9 or 12 months.
Service: Call 800-231-0900 for a list of service centers. There is no hotline for troubleshooting because they aim to make the dealers

the focal point for all inquiries. Dealers are required to carry spare parts for every computer at all times.
Technical Manuals: None.

Corona Data Systems, 275 East Hillcrest Drive, Thousand Oaks, CA 91360.
Warranty: 90 days parts and labor.
Extended Service Policy: None.
Service: Sold and serviced through computer stores or through any Xerox center (Xerox owns Corona). For troubleshooting information call 800-621-6746.
Technical Manuals: Available through dealers.

Franklin Computers, 1070 Busch Memorial Highway, Pennsauken, NJ 08110.
Warranty: 90 days (units) and 1 year (disk drives) parts and labor.
Extended Service Policy: Available through stores or through Bell & Howell.
Service: Available through authorized dealers, directly through Franklin, or through a Bell & Howell depot. Call 609-488-0600 (ask for the Technical Service Department) for locations of authorized dealers or Bell & Howell depots.
Technical Manuals: Available through Franklin.

IBM, Entry Systems Division, P.O. Box 1328, Boca Raton, FL 33432.
Warranty: 90 days parts and labor for PC and PC/XT; 1 year parts and labor for PCjr, Portable Personal Computer, and PC AT.
Extended Service Policy: A variety of policies is available for all products, including on-site and carry-in coverage.
Service: Available from IBM Service Centers and through a variety of independent dealers. Call 800-428-2569 for locations.
Technical Manuals: Available from IBM Product Centers.

NEC, 1414 Massachusetts Avenue, Boxborough, MA 01719.
Warranty: 90 days parts and labor.
Extended Service Policy: Prices range from 10 to 12 percent of retail price.
Service: Dealers to do their own maintenance and sell extended

service policies. Some provide on-site repair. Hourly rate of $65 for hardware repairs.
Technical Manuals: Available through dealers.

Radio Shack, One Tandy Center, Fort Worth, TX 76102.
Warranty: 90 days parts and labor.
Extended Service Policy: Available through Radio Shack.
Service: Available only through authorized Radio Shack stores.

Texas Instruments, 12501 Research, Mailstop 2222, Austin, TX 78759.
Warranty: 90 days parts and labor.
Extended Service Policy: Various policies available from Texas Instruments.
Service: Available from TI-authorized dealers; call 800-527-3300 for details.
Technical Manuals: Available from TI; call 800-847-2787 for parts and manuals.

Zenith Data Systems, St. Joseph, Michigan 49022.
Warranty: 90 days parts and labor.
Extended Service Policy: Available through dealers, not Zenith.
Service: Call 800-842-9000 for location of Zenith-authorized service centers. Some do on-site repairs.
Technical Manuals: Available directly from Zenith at above address.

PRINTERS

Diablo Systems, 901 Page Road, P.O. Box 5030, Fremont, CA 94537.
Warranty: 90 days parts and labor.
Extended Service Policy: Variety of policies available from Diablo.
Service: Through Diablo and Xerox Americare. Call 415-498-4009 for troubleshooting and service center locations.
Technical Manuals: Available through Diablo.

Epson America, 3415 Kahiwa Street, Torrance, CA 90505.
Warranty: 90 days parts and labor.
Extended Service Policy: Call 213-539-9140 for details.
Service: Available directly from Epson or from authorized service centers.
Technical Manuals: Available from Epson at above number.

Juki Industries of America, 299 Market Street, Saddle Brook, NJ 07662.
Warranty: 90 days parts and labor.
Extended Service Policy: One-year contracts available through Xerox Americare.
Service: Call 201-368-3666 for a list of authorized service centers.

Leading Edge Products, 225 Turnpike Street, Canton, MA 02021.
Warranty: One year parts and labor.
Extended Service Policy: Not available from Leading Edge, but some dealers offer extended service policies.
Service: Approximately 550 repair centers. Call 800-343-6857 for troubleshooting and service locations.
Technical Manuals: Available through the "800" number above.

NEC, 44 Cummings Park, Woburn, MA 01801.
Warranty: 90 days parts and labor.
Extended Service Policy: One-year maintenance plans available.
Service: Call 800-325-5500 for a list of service centers. There are three types of service available: carry-in at certain locations; on-site available within 100 miles of 75 nationwide service centers; mail-in to factory.
Technical Manuals: Maintenance guides may be ordered through the above "800" number.

Okidata, 532 Fellowship Road, Mount Laurel, NJ 08054.
Warranty: 90 days parts and labor (printer), 1 year (print head); extended warranty available within 10 days of purchase.
Extended Service Policy: One-year policy available from dealer or Okidata. Policy must be purchased within 90 days of printer purchase.

Service: Okidata maintains regional service depots plus 3,600 authorized service centers, many of which are dealers. Call 800-OKIDATA for locations.

Qume Corporation, 2350 Qume Drive, San Jose, CA 95131.
Warranty: 6 months parts and labor.
Extended Service Policy: Available through General Electric.
Service: Warranty service available through either GE or Qume. Call 800-446-6400 for locations.
Technical Manuals: Available through the above "800" number.

Silver-Reed Corporation, 19600 South Vermont Avenue, Torrance, CA 90502.
Warranty: 90 days parts and labor.
Extended Service Policy: Available only for 500 and 550 models through Xerox Americare. Not available for 400 and 770 models.
Service: Available through dealers (who contact distributors for servicing). All distributors provide service. Call 800-421-4191 for technical information.
Technical Manuals: Service manuals available through the "800" number above.

Star Micronics, 2803 E. 12th Street, Dallas/Fort Worth Airport, TX 75261.
Warranty: 90 days parts and labor.
Extended Service Policy: None available.
Service: Through authorized dealers; call 714-768-4340 for information.
Technical Manuals: Available from Star Micronics at above number.

Transtar, Vivitar Computer Products, P.O. Box C-96975, Bellevue, WA 98009.
Warranty: 6 months parts and labor.
Extended Service Policy: None available.
Service: Available through authorized service centers.
Technical Manuals: Available directly from Transtar.

MODEMS

Hayes Microcomputer Products, 5923 Peachtree Industrial Blvd., Norcross, GA 30092.
Warranty: 2 years parts and labor.
Extended Service Policy: None.
Service: Call 800-241-6492 for troubleshooting and service locations.
Technical Manuals: None.

Novation, 20409 Prairie Street, Chatsworth, CA 91311.
Warranty: 2 years parts and labor.
Extended Service Policy: None available.
Service: Call 800-423-5419 (in Calif., 213-966-5060) for authorized locations.
Technical Manuals: None available.

Transend, 2190 Paragon Drive, San Jose, CA 95131.
Warranty: 2 years parts and labor.
Extended Service Policy: None.
Service: Available only from Transend. Call 408-946-7400 to obtain a "return authorization number" before sending modem. If not covered under warranty, hourly rate is $20 plus parts.
Technical Manuals: None.

INDEX

ABOUT THE AUTHORS

JOEL MAKOWER is a Washington, D.C.–based writer, editor, and president of Tilden Press, Inc., a book-packaging company. He is the author of *Office Hazards: How Your Job Can Make You Sick* (Tilden Press, 1981), which investigates the health effects of modern office environments, and *Personal Computers A–Z* (Quantum Press/ Doubleday, 1984). A native of Oakland, California, he is a graduate in journalism of the University of California at Berkeley.

As a college freshman, ED MURRAY got lost on campus and ended up in the university computer center. From there he began a twenty-year fascination with computer hardware and software. He is currently president of MetaFont, Inc., a firm engaged in the development of microcomputer-based publishing, typesetting, and media conversion software systems. He lives in Arlington, Virginia.